Books by Daniel Callahan

THE NEW CHURCH

THE SECULAR CITY DEBATE (*editor*)

GENERATION OF THE THIRD EYE (*editor*)

HONESTY IN THE CHURCH

FEDERAL AID AND CATHOLIC SCHOOLS (*editor*)

THE MIND OF THE CATHOLIC LAYMAN

CHRISTIANITY DIVIDED: PROTESTANT AND ROMAN
   CATHOLIC THEOLOGICAL ISSUES (*co-editor*)

The New Church

THE
NEW CHURCH
Essays in Catholic Reform

DANIEL CALLAHAN

CHARLES SCRIBNER'S SONS · New York

62492

ACKNOWLEDGMENTS

This collection could not have been published but for the kindness of the
editors of the various journals and publishers of books in which these essays
first appeared. I wish to express my thanks for their cooperation.

"Alienation and Response" (Copyright © 1960 Daniel Callahan),
Commonweal, April 8, 1960.

"Politics and Catholic Authority" (Copyright © 1960 Daniel Callahan),
Christianity and Crisis, October 3, 1960, under the title, "Freedom and
Authority in Roman Catholicism."

"The Lay Revolution" (Copyright © 1962 Daniel Callahan), Commonweal, August 10, 1962, under the title, "Problems and Possibilities."

"Confronting Protestantism" (Copyright © 1959 Daniel Callahan),
Commonweal, September 18, 1959, under the title, "A Leap of Faith."

"The Legacy of Pio Nono" (Copyright © 1965 Daniel Callahan), The
Critic, October–November 1965.

"The New Pluralism" (Copyright © 1963 Daniel Callahan), Commonweal, September 6, 1963.

The opposite page constitutes an extension of the copyright page.

FOR
Paul and Rose Mary Desjardins

On Collecting Essays

A book of collected essays is, in the best of circumstances, a happenstance matter. The first problem lies in the essays themselves. Unless they are very long, their writing rarely gives an author the chance to develop his thoughts fully. Somewhat like an insatiable bee, he moves from one flower to the next, drawing drops of honey from all but rarely taking the measure of any. A second problem is that essays can lose their contextual point very quickly. Most of those collected here were written on request, often in response to the appearance of certain problems or books on the religious or cultural scene. A third problem is that of organizing disparate essays into some kind of coherent whole.

There is not much an author can do, after the fact, to fill in the gaps present in his essays. He could of course simply expand each one, but short of starting all over, this is not easily done. With the exception of a few stylistic changes, I have let the essays stand as they appeared. There are occasional passages I would now like to change, but I think one just has to live with one's past, resisting the temptation to censor the earlier self, a self which, after all, once existed and which still continues to impress its mark on the present self. Fortunately, a collection can help a bit toward redressing any unhappy balances. As will become clear there are a number of themes to which I return again and again. This is sometimes hard on my occasional delusion of self-consistency, but it often turns out that some excess in one article has been corrected by an excess in the other direction in still another article! Taken together, these excesses do help to delineate the framework within which my mind has worked.

As for the selection of essays, I have presented in this book only those pieces which still say things I want to say, even if their initial occasion has now passed. This is especially true of the essays in Part I, which I have entitled "Early Tensions." All four were written between 1959 and 1962, those fearful and expectant years just prior to the opening of Vatican II. I include them here because they represent, in my own development, a setting of the stage. But not just my own stage. I believe that in their concerns, dilemmas, and uncertainties, they represent a kind of probing which has remained with many others up until the very present. At any rate, they show where I started and what I felt had to be done. The rest of the book represents my own way of coming to grips, in one setting or another, with most of those central concerns. I have reserved for the final chapter some brief observations on what I think has happened, not only to me but also to many others, in the intervening years.

The problem of organizing the essays proved particularly difficult. I have never managed to keep my different interests isolated from each other, nor have I tried. Certain groupings, however, seemed reasonably sensible, though here and there different essays could just as legitimately have been included in different sections. Some repetitions were, I am afraid, unavoidable, but I hope the reader can tolerate them, or at least take them as a clue to the kinds of issues which have attached themselves to me like burrs.

A final word. Just as these essays vary in their subject matter, they also vary in their length and gravity, their style and tone. This was inevitable, given the different circumstances under which they were written, the different audiences to whom they were directed, and the different moods which beset me as I wrote them. It would be a mistake, however, to think that the shorter articles, or those superficially more "popular," necessarily reflect opinions and conclusions more lightly held. As may well happen with other writers and scholars, very short articles have often forced me to a directness and clarity which escaped my grasp in longer pieces replete with scholarly apparatus. I have always been skeptical of the disdain some solemn people express at the thought of doing short essays. The argument is that one just can't say enough, or work in the necessary nuances and details in anything less than a full-fledged monograph or book. They have a point. But I have always felt that if someone has something worth saying, he could with only modest writing skills manage to get his main points across in a short space. Whether I have shown it can be done, or whether I have anything to say, I must leave to the judgment of others.

It would be remiss not to thank my wife, Sidney, for her help in putting this collection together. She had to listen to me talk about these essays before I wrote them, listen some more while I tried to write them, read them once published, discuss the public reaction to them, and then, burden of burdens, start all over again for the sake of this collection. Only a devoted wife could take up that kind of cross. And only a sensible wife could, by a delicately raised eyebrow and a faint trace of doubt in her voice, tell me in no uncertain terms which essays should not be included. In every case, I took the hint and for that the reader can be thankful.

DANIEL CALLAHAN

Contents

The New Church

PART I

Early Tensions
1959-1962

CHAPTER ONE

Alienation and Response

LABELING IS A DANGEROUS BUSINESS. HOW THE FUTURE HISTORIAN
will label the present age of the Church in America is impossible
to say. Still, there are two labels given to our time which would
apply unusually well to contemporary American Catholic intellectual life. I am thinking of Morton White's characterization of ours
as an "Age of Analysis" and W. H. Auden's complementary description of ours as an "Age of Anxiety." Nothing has been more pronounced in the recent literature on Catholic intellectualism than
the absence of visionary schemes and grandiose plans for the future.
The greatest part of the effort has gone into close analyses of our
historical and sociological origins and detailed critiques of our
faults, assets, and potentialities. But to say that the present generation is analytic is to tell only half the story. For this analysis has
been induced by an acute sense of anxiety about our deficiencies
and a fundamental uncertainty about the future role of the Catholic
intellectual.

Curiously, little has been written about the mentality of the contemporary Catholic intellectual. We have been told what his role in the past has been, what his role in the future ought to be. We have a fairly clear picture, statistically, of what he is doing and not doing. Such statistics, however, give only fragmentary clues to what historians sometimes call the "spirit" of a people. In this instance, the "spirit" of the Catholic intellectual in America can only be guessed vaguely from the things he has written about himself. In a sense this is to say the obvious. Yet the implications of the obvious are obscure. There is no way of telling how the majority of Catholic intellectuals are, in fact, adjusting themselves psychologically to the dual demands of Church and society. Is the Catholic responding to the exhortations for a revived Catholic intellectual life or has the die already been cast in another form? What is the society in which he lives, particularly its intellectual life, doing to him—to the way he thinks about himself and conceives his role? How, in short, is he adjusting the demands and values of society to the demands and needs of the Church? This last question is central. What the Catholic intellectual is or comes to be will be a function of the way he personally solves the problem of adjusting to demands often at variance with each other.

It is possible already to make some tentative observations about the forms these adjustments are coming to take. The concerns of the non-Catholic intellectual world, for instance, are increasingly Catholic concerns, its tensions and musings, the Catholic's tensions and musings. As the walls of parochialism tumble, piece by piece, the common questions in society become more gripping and the general mood and temper more pervasive. Above all, the Catholic intellectual wants to find a place for himself in the broader discussions and debates. To take one small example of how this is being done, the number of Catholics in non-Catholic academic societies is increasing rapidly. We still have the American Catholic Philosophical, Historical, and Sociology Associations and they are not likely to disappear. But more and more members of those associations are becoming members also of their non-Catholic counterpart associations. More significantly, a considerable number of Catholic scholars will not join the Catholic associations at all. To this group, the very fact of separate Catholic professional societies merely fosters the separation these very societies spend so much of their time deploring at their conventions.

One is tempted to say that the pattern of the Catholic intellectual in America is beginning to approximate that of his counterpart in Europe in his sensitivity to non-Catholic thought. In the past, the American Catholic pattern was one of framing its own questions in response to the internal needs of the Church. These needs were often simply a matter of survival and bare existence, whether intellectual, moral, or social existence. What Catholic intellectual life there was most often originated from the necessity of meeting challenges and attacks from intellectual and social movements outside the Church. If anything new was developed, it was often the result of the prick provided by external stimuli. This meant—and still means—a general intellectual lag. By the time Catholic intellectuals got around to responding to the dynamic currents in American intellectual circles, these movements were often on the wane. Even today it is rare for Catholics to be in at the start of broad intellectual developments. Only when these developments become threats or unavoidable issues do we respond. The very fact that so much of our talk of Catholic intellectualism is couched in the language of "meeting challenges," "countering threats," "taking our place," and so on indicates that initiative and foresight are not our strong points. Naturally, much of this can be explained sociologically and historically. But no one has yet shown how a separate system of higher education, scholarly journals, publishing houses, and intellectual societies can overcome separation and cease to hinder assimilation.

This has not been the case for some time in Europe. Although there are Catholic universities, journals, and societies, the intellectual life of the Catholic is better integrated with that of the non-Catholic. The average Catholic intellectual in Europe has attended the same schools, for a time at least, as his non-Catholic peer, reads the same journals, and participates in the same broad intellectual circles. The majority of Catholic philosophers in England, for example, have had their undergraduate or graduate training at Oxford or Cambridge or have done some work at one or the other. The non-Catholics who have shaped contemporary English philosophy are men who were once their professors, their friends, and their associates. While the philosophical conclusions of Catholics may differ radically from their non-Catholic colleagues, one finds in their writing the same language being used, the same technical problems being analyzed, and the same undercurrents at work. This is not to say that English Catholic philosophers feel themselves to be part and parcel of English philosophy. Far from it. But in comparison with the situation of the American Catholic philosopher they are well advanced.

In our country, on the contrary, as the Catholic intellectual tries to work his way out of the ghetto there is little ground on which to build. Like all newcomers to any established society, he is neither fully at home in the new world nor happy with the narrower world he is trying to move beyond. He is even more an alien in American intellectual life than he is in the broader social and political life. If he is at all successful in finding a place in the established secular order, he is likely to do so only at the cost of alienating himself from the Catholic milieu he must in part abandon. Both Catholics and non-Catholics are likely to see him as something of an anomaly: the less venturesome Catholic may consider him a fellow-traveler of secularism while the non-Catholic may consider him a fifth-column agent of Catholic power. The general non-Catholic opinion that a Catholic cannot be a genuine intellectual and the native Catholic suspicion of the American intelligentsia suggest the dimensions of the problem.

The difficulties the Catholic faces in being accepted in the non-Catholic intellectual world are real enough. The doubts that many Americans feel about Catholics are, if anything, intensified among intellectuals. A long heritage of separation is not quickly overcome. Yet this is just one side of the coin, only half the alienation problem. Sharply put, popular American Catholic culture frequently causes the Catholic intellectual considerable agony, chagrin, and frustration. It is a culture not of his making, a culture not greatly influenced by his work, a culture not altogether sure of his value. In few instances is it a culture that shares his non-religious goals, his aesthetic, social, or political tastes. With rare exceptions most of the characteristic patterns of American Catholicism were shaped by different generations to meet different needs, and these patterns still dominate our parishes, societies, and universities. Small wonder the Catholic intellectual feels isolated and out of step even in his own religious community.

His training, temper, and role impel the intellectual to judge the American Church in its actual cultural and sociological manifestations. He is forced to accept some strains of this culture, to reject others, to laud some of its spokesmen, to decry and work against the influence of others. He must make a thousand and one distinctions which do not trouble other Catholics at all. Worse still, if he does achieve some degree of assimilation into non-Catholic intellectual circles, he is likely to see the weaknesses of the Church with new eyes. He is likely to be a good bit more critical and sensitive about trends in American Catholicism which seem to bear out the objection that the Catholic intellectual is a contradiction in terms. And of course when he does become critical of American Catholicism, he may be accused by fellow Catholics of having his judgment distorted by secularism. To complete the picture, the non-Catholic intellectual is tempted to dismiss the Catholic intellectual as the exception proving the rule when he learns that he is not completely acceptable in his own camp.

It would be astounding in this kind of situation if the Catholic intellectual did not find his life trying, ambiguous, and shot through with tensions and uncertainties. Both the Catholic and the non-Catholic world want his full allegiance—not one foot in one camp and one in another. But the very nature of the intellectual life demands a repudiation of the party spirit. The "intellectual" who sees his task as one of using his mind exclusively to further the interests of his party, faction, or even church hardly deserves the name. This, unfortunately, is what he is expected to do. It is easy enough to talk in the abstract about the duties and responsibilities of the intellectual life. It is far harder to put them into practice in the concrete realities of life. For the Catholic intellectual, it is sometimes incredibly difficult to distinguish between the service of truth and the service of partisanship.

It is a very rare Catholic intellectual who doesn't manage to compromise himself in one way or other. The desire to rid oneself of the tensions generated by the intellectual life can be overwhelming. Two extreme ways of resolving conflict are worth noting. At one extreme is the suppression of embarrassment and alienation by violently repudiating what is non-Catholic: to "spit one's Catholicism in the face of secularists" as one ardent soul described his mode of adjustment. Another extreme is to repudiate American Catholic culture, to dissociate oneself from all that smacks of the popular, the old, and the traditional in American Catholicism. A psychoanalyst might describe these two radical alternatives as different, but related, ways of resolving inner stress: the one by turning aggression outward, the other by turning it inward. If neither of these extremes is common in a pure state, it is difficult not to succumb in some degree to one or the other from time to time. There are traces of both in our recent self-criticism as well as in the objection voiced by many that we don't need any self-criticism. Neither of these extreme responses is unusual among minority groups, Catholic or non-Catholic. On the ethnic level, every minority in this country has had its share of members who work off their frustrations by rigid defensiveness or outright repudiation of what they are taken to represent. This is no less true of the intellectual as a minority group.

Rarely is the work of the intellectual appreciated and understood. Too often in America the intellectual has been accused of disloyalty and subversion. He *has* been disloyal: to the status quo, to the popular mores and fads, and to the jingoistic values taken to be true Americanism. So too, he has frequently been provincial in defending America against the attacks of European intellectuals. Analogously, the American Catholic intellectual occupies a comparable position within the American Church. He *is* often disloyal in the same (and good) sense but he too is capable, on occasion, of succumbing to ecclesiastical chauvinism. The analogy can be pushed a step further. As the American intellectual (until very recently) found much of his inspiration in European thought, so too the Catholic intellectual is often forced to turn to European Catholicism for his inspiration. While this inspiration may save the day for the Catholic, it makes it all the more difficult for him to adjust himself to the American scene. And the folks back home, often quite satisfied with the progress of the Church in America, are rarely happy when he holds up for emulation German or French Catholicism.

It might be comforting if we could believe that the alienation of the Catholic intellectual in America is just a temporary matter which will lessen with the passage of time. It is just beginning, for the conditions which create it are really only beginning. That is, we are now entering a long transition period in which more and more Catholic intellectuals will seek to break down the wall of separation between themselves and American intellectual life. Undeniably, there will always be some fundamental differences which will divide us, as Catholics, from our non-Catholic brother. No less certain is the fact that the Catholic intellectual—if he does his proper work— will continue to collide with forces hostile to him within the Church. It has never been otherwise in the history of the Church. In America we have just begun the attempt to integrate ourselves into the broad intellectual life around us. The initial phase is troublesome enough; increased integration will bring more, not fewer, problems. The reason for this is, I think, evident. It is far simpler for the Catholic intellectual to achieve recognition and status either within or outside of the Church than it is for him to know how to serve both Church and world at the same time. We have been told we ought to achieve integration; we do not yet understand how this will be possible.

CHAPTER TWO

Politics and Catholic Authority

WHATEVER ELSE MAY BE SAID ABOUT CATHOLICISM AND THE Presidency, no one is now likely to deny its importance as an issue in the 1960 election. Yet John F. Kennedy, most will agree, did all that was possible to reassure the doubtful and the skeptical. His solemn pledge, repeated many times, that he would tolerate no ecclesiastical pressure or direction in fulfilling his oath of office was as much as he or anyone in his position could do.

But if no doubt lingered about Mr. Kennedy's intention to be independent, considerable doubt seemed to remain about the theoretical legitimacy, for a Catholic, of the kind of pledge that he made. The assumption, for instance, of a statement issued by the "National Conference of Citizens for Religious Freedom" was that good intentions would not suffice in the face of (inevitably) strong pressure from the Catholic hierarchy. How could they suffice when, according to the statement, "his church insists that he is

10

duty-bound to admit to its direction"? This particular doubt was apparently justified by the celebrated *L'Osservatore Romano* editorial of May 19, 1960, "Firm Points." Among other things the editorial asserted the duty of the laity to show a "dutiful discipline" when the bishops speak out about political matters that "touch the altar."

Yet Mr. Kennedy simply shrugged off the editorial and repeated his pledge. Nor was he alone. To a man, the American Catholic commentators on the editorial denied its relevancy or application to Mr. Kennedy or to the American situation and seriously questioned the firmness of the points themselves.

Still, as so often happens, reassurances and clarification about a specific incident do comparatively little to illuminate permanent principles. This incident had a familiar, almost classic, air about it: the severe Roman statement of obscure authority, a shocked and irritated American Catholic reaction, a hasty clarification in Rome, and a spate of diocesan editorials drawing numerous "necessary distinctions." In the end, naturally, few were much the wiser about Roman Catholic teaching on the matters in question and still less about the nature of Roman Catholic authority.

In fact, the whole discussion occasioned by Mr. Kennedy's candidacy has done little to clarify: (a) the sources of Catholic teaching, (b) the nature of hierarchical authority over the layman, or (c) the relationship of practice to principle. What has been revealed, particularly in the area of Church and State, is that American Catholics are themselves divided on the theoretical significance of special teachings in the past, but are united in believing that they are as free as any other American in supporting the Constitution. By now, however, I think many American Catholics (and European Catholics in similar situations) are aware that their assertion of loyalty and the pledges of their bishops do appear to fly in the face of much that was once taken as the doctrine of the Church. Even though the Catholic does feel that there is much that theoretically supports his traditional American practice, he is aware that there are still gaps in Catholic theology and unresolved doctrinal disputes. If we Catholics have succeeded in making clear that, say, the Spanish Church is not normative for Catholicism, we have not succeeded in making clear what is.

The practical harm (though accidental) done by this uncertainty, by these doctrinal lacunae, by these internal Catholic debates, is greater than it ought to be and customarily is. It is understandably difficult for the non-Catholic to know which Catholic spokesman he can trust in such a situation. And no perceptive Catholic can fail to be aware of the inherent difficulty of attempting to prove that his good intentions are supported by Catholic doctrine when some other Catholic may attack his understanding of the doctrine.

For the Catholic himself, nevertheless, it is usually of no great moment that other Catholics will disagree with him or even attack him. More painful is the fact that many non-Catholics are apt to see these disputes not as empirical evidence of Catholic diversity and freedom but as evidence that one side or another in any dispute can be assumed to be heterodox; and that all one need do to determine which is to skim through ancient or recent encyclicals, allocutions, or diocesan editorials, tally sheet in hand, looking for passages that agree or disagree with the disputed propositions. The Catholic too does this—but not entirely and not in such literal fashion.

Now it would be extremely useful if the Catholic could present a neat, detailed guide to the structure and nature of Church authority. With such a guide it might be possible to resolve some of the misunderstandings that arise concerning the freedom of the Catholic or the value to be assigned a specific statement by Pope or bishop. But there is no such precise guide, nor is there ever likely to be one. Even to wish there were one would, I think, betray a fundamental misunderstanding of Church authority as the Catholic sees it.

There are, to be sure, numerous descriptions of the teaching and disciplinary authority of the Church and the hierarchy couched in general language to be found in Catholic manuals of ecclesiology. It is certainly true, for instance, that every Catholic is bound to accept the teaching of the Church as declared by the popes and councils. It is equally true that the Catholic is bound to respect the direction and guidance of his bishop in matters of faith and morals. Yet having said this (or anything of like abstractness), one has not said anything very helpful for dealing with specific teachings, pronouncements, or directives.

First of all, given a specific statement there will be the problem of determining the kind of assent it requires. All teachings are not equally binding, all pronouncements are not equally solemn; some will require simple obedience while others will require internal assent to their truth as well. What is true of papal statements holds good even more strongly of episcopal statements.

Secondly, there will often be some question about the meaning of the statement, especially in those instances in which it must be harmonized with other statements on the same subject. With respect to meaning, it will always be necessary to determine the circumstances under which it was uttered, the persons to whom it was addressed, and all that might be called the "literary form" of the statement.

Thirdly, if the utterance has some potential bearing on conduct, there will be questions about the prudential implications. It is a rare statement, pronouncement, or teaching that does not occasion discussion and analysis on all three levels and often enough a plethora of different interpretations.

One may, if so inclined, look upon distinctions of this kind as the rankest kind of legalism and the freedom they permit as more illusory than real. For the Catholic they loom large and are unavoidable, since the individual Catholic and the Church exist in the most diverse cultures and traditions. The Church expects that the individual Catholic will make the necessary distinctions and that there will be honest and legitimate differences from nation to nation and from individual to individual. Given this situation and this expectation it is extremely difficult to deduce from any abstract definition of Catholic authority the specific weight of a given papal or episcopal statement. This is not to say that Catholics do not attempt such deductions; quite evidently we do. It is still never an easy matter and differing deductions are the cause of some of the sharpest theological debates.

Without multiplying the formal complexities and ambiguities of Catholic authority any further, I think I have said enough to indicate why the Catholic invariably finds it difficult to state to what exactly he is bound. What I have said should also indicate why, on occasion, the Catholic can differ so sharply from the non-Catholic about the meaning of the Church's teaching. The very nature and practice of Catholic authority presuppose that the individual has a conscience, a mind, and a free will, and that it is his obligation to respect them. In no instance may the Catholic violate his conscience. In every instance he must think and make a personal decision. Precisely these requirements—in the eyes of the Catholic—distinguish the system of Catholic authority from that of either a military system or a totalitarian government. This is not to say that the Catholic who holds a minority opinion on some matter or other will avoid unpopularity or attack; it is to say that one can *never* judge either the Catholic or his position on that basis alone or infer *only* from the number who support his position whether such a position is compatible with Catholic doctrine.

Now if it is not a simple matter to provide the non-Catholic with the key to Catholic authority (for the Catholic himself possesses no single key), it is possible to suggest an indirect way of reaching some viable conclusions about specific issues and specific pronouncements. That way is simply this: that one observe the decision-making process of Catholics themselves and of regional or national Catholic communities.

To do this, the following kinds of questions are helpful. (1) How does a Catholic determine what the teaching of the Church is? (2) How does a specific Catholic community decide to what it is bound and to what it is not bound? (3) How does a Catholic whose views have been attacked by other Catholics decide whether his position is a tenable or legitimate one to hold? What these questions have in common is that they assume that one good way to determine what Catholic doctrines consist of is by asking what Catholics *take* them to be and to mean. Proceeding in this fashion, a fairly rough but accurate answer can be given to these questions.

Catholics are likely to be guided quite as much by what they take to be the behavior and attitude of the Church as they see it around them as they are by formally stated teachings and pronouncements. This means that Catholics, when confronted by what *looks* to be an authoritative statement or command, will under normal circumstances clarify any doubts by looking to the local consensus of opinion for the interpretation of the teaching as well as its status. Now this way of resolving doubts can be misleading at times, and it is always conceivable that a local consensus may be at odds with the universal teaching of the Church. Many Southern Catholics were apparently, until recently, under the impression that the Church approved of racial discrimination. Only repeated condemnations by numerous Southern bishops, reproof from the Holy Office, and a look at the national Catholic consensus were able (one hopes!) to convince them of their mistake. Yet even allowing for confusion and error over a small area, the possibility of such error over a large area becomes very unlikely.

In any event, there is no way more appropriate for a Catholic to learn the meaning and import of a purported doctrine than by questioning those entrusted with the task of teaching and instructing: the bishops, priests, and theologians. The layman, in looking to the bishops in particular for clarification, will be guided as much by silence as by positive statements. If the bishops have not specifically condemned a position held by prominent Catholics (assuming they are aware that some Catholics do hold the position), the presumption on the part of the Catholic is that they are free to hold the view even though they may know the bishops do not personally agree with the position. Put another way, a consensus of Catholic opinion is generally the best way to determine what Catholics take the Church to teach and demand of them. *But* a tolerant silence on the part of the hierarchy is, normally, good evidence that a Catholic is free to hold a minority position.

For just that reason nothing is quite so misleading as the common expression "official Catholic position." And the mistake is simply compounded when particular Catholics (including Presidential candidates) or groups of Catholics are summarily dismissed as genuine Catholics solely on the grounds that other Catholics have attacked them or that they represent a minority viewpoint. The mistake borders on the incredible when it is suggested that the entire American hierarchy has repudiated the teaching of the Church by pledging to support now and in the future the separation of Church and State and the maintenance of religious toleration.

So far then, in a very rough fashion, I have indicated how the Catholic himself will make decisions about the teaching of the Church and the extent and limits of the freedom permitted him. The Catholic response to the *L'Osservatore Romano* editorial does, I think, offer a pertinent illustration of some of the suggested approaches.

Without laboring the obvious fact that this paper is not a teaching organ of the Church, the real question is not whether *that* statement can be taken as "authoritative" or not. Its form and place preclude such a possibility. Rather, the real question is simply whether the view expressed in the editorial is a reasonably accurate summary of Catholic teaching that can be found expressed more definitively and precisely elsewhere. Now by the method I have suggested, the general Catholic response to and interpretation of the editorial will be a major test by which the Catholic will decide whether the viewpoint stated there is the teaching of the Church. What was the response?

From all sides, the response was one of dismay, anger, and embarrassment. With varying degrees of vehemence, the comments that appeared in European and American periodicals were those of strong reservation. All accepted the general principle expressed in the editorial, that "it is absurd to split the conscience into one part which is that of the believer and one which is that of the citizen." But few accepted all of the concrete implications that the editorial drew from the general principle.

Noteworthy, however, was the fact that the commentators were themselves vague and imprecise about exactly *which* implications they could not accept as consonant with their understanding of Catholic teaching. Instead of specifically denying specific points, most chose to center their complaint on the carelessness of the wording of the editorial and its failure to emphasize the freedom of the Catholic in political and civic life. Most objected also to the failure of the writer to take account of the effect of the editorial outside Italy.

Now as useful as it is to know that most Catholics objected to the editorial and denied its importance or accuracy, one could hardly say that the responses were very informative about the basic issues raised by the editorial. If the editorial was, at some critical points, wrong about Catholic teaching, what is the correct teaching? The consensus, for all its vagueness, revealed that few think Catholic teaching requires the kind of "dutiful discipline" the editorial claimed. No less escapable is the conclusion that no one was willing to claim the Catholic can simply ignore the hierarchy in public and civic life. This may seem a very meager conclusion, if not nebulous and evasive. I submit it is neither in one important sense.

That sense is this. Implicit in my description of Catholic authority is the assumption that, insofar as it can be called a system, it is a system that strives to balance legitimate claims on the part of the Church and inherent human rights. The non-Catholic will doubtless see the scale as unevenly weighted. In practice it sometimes is. Yet what the consensus sketched above shows is a recognition of the necessity and validity of such a balance. Specifically, it shows that the Catholic does not believe the Church requires anything of him which would deprive him of his freedom as a citizen or person.

CHAPTER THREE

The Lay Revolution

I T IS IMPOSSIBLE TO TALK ABOUT THE STATUS OF THE LAITY IN THE Church today without talking about the relationship of laity and clergy. Yet however one chooses to characterize that relationship, one is bound to be struck by a number of curiosities. The most patent in recent years was the establishment by Pope John XXIII of a preparatory commission on the lay apostolate for the forthcoming Council. For the first time in the history of the Church, the question of the laity had been given a status equal to that of the traditional matters which have concerned ecumenical councils. But it very soon became clear that no provisions were to be made for lay consultants or advisers to that commission.

The commission thus had the curious distinction that it was the only one in which none of those who will be affected directly by its work were represented. A theological commission without theologians or a commission on the missions without missionaries would have been unthinkable. In contrast, hardly a word was spoken about the omission of laymen from the deliberations of the preparatory commission on the laity; it was accepted as a matter of course. One need hardly add that no laymen will be participants in the Council itself.

No one, of course, is surprised by these omissions. For many centuries the layman has had no direct role to play in the highest deliberations of the Church. Neither Canon Law nor recent tradition encourages such a role. If the very fact that a commission on the laity was formed is revolutionary, the exclusion of the laity from it is merely the faithful following of modern tradition. The importance of the laity was dramatically recognized; the importance of the contribution they might make in a preparatory commission was not.

This combination of revolution in one direction and close adherence to custom in another perfectly symbolizes the problem of the laity in the Church today. For the problem is one which goes well beyond the usual diagnoses and appraisals. It is not only, as is often said, a matter of the clergy becoming less paternalistic, less authoritarian, and more open to the needs and talents of the laity. Nor is it only a matter of stimulating the laity to be more active and energetic in serving the Church. To be sure, all these things are needed. But what is needed even more is a sharp awareness that, as the Church is structured today, none of those advances would guarantee a viable and integral place for the laity. None, moreover, would guarantee that awakening lay aspirations would fully be met.

To put it directly, the Church is in the midst of a revolution with which it does not have the means, juridical or theological, to cope. The revolution has been long in the making—both clergy and laity have contributed to bringing it about. From the clerical side, the innumerable exhortations of recent popes that the laity become more active in the service of the Church, the work of important clerics on the theology of the laity, and the widespread desire of many bishops, pastors, and priests for lay assistance have been a major influence. From the lay side, the emergence of an educated class of laymen, the heeding of papal and episcopal words, and a general rebirth of Christian spirituality have all made a profound difference. Taken together, these developments are nothing less than revolutionary.

But what has been the result of this ferment? Very little, it would appear. For the most part the revolution remains one of attitude, expectation, and aspiration—not one of profound change in the Church itself. The Church, it becomes increasingly obvious, is not geared for this comparatively sudden development. For decades the Church's organizational and institutional life has been the sole responsibility of the clergy: from the teaching office of the Church down to the most remote parish everything of importance has been in the hands of the clergy. The absence of laymen from the preparatory commission on the laity simply typifies, in a singular fashion, the present relationship of laity and clergy. Even in those matters which directly concern the laity, the laity are, for the most part, not consulted.

The one conclusion that ought not to be drawn from these facts is that the hierarchy and clergy are engaged in a great conspiracy to keep the layman in his place. This is hardly reasonable, hardly fair. It is much more to the point to recognize how centuries of custom have brought about the present situation; to recognize, that is, that the present generation of clergy (and laity) has been nurtured and shaped by a long tradition of seeing the laity as inactive, decidedly silent, members of the Church. Even more to the point, there is little in Canon Law which would appear to sanction the laity's playing a fuller role in the Church. Canonically, there is little to encourage the clergy to give the laity more freedom and responsibility; there is simply no provision at all for the layman to exercise some special role of his own.

Indeed, I think it particularly necessary to recognize that Canon Law spells out in great detail the duties and obligations of the clergy; it scarcely mentions the rights of the laity. The effect of this one-sided stress is to offer little in the way of encouragement to the priest or bishop who might feel inclined to grant greater independence to the laymen under his jurisdiction; the major responsibilities are his and he is the one accountable.

Caution, under these circumstances, is only natural. Nothing enjoins the clergy to delegate responsibility; on the contrary, almost everything enjoins him not to, if only as the course of care and prudence. The inevitable outcome of this canonical situation has been merely to reinforce historical and sociological trends: the isolation of seminary training, the social and educational gap between laity and clergy, and the development of a paternalistic attitude on the part of the clergy and one of passivity on the part of the laity.

This is not to say that the clergy could not do more than they already do; clearly they could. But it does suggest that the supposed tension existing between laity and clergy can easily be misunderstood—if only because there are so many priests who do want the laity to take a more active role. Yet their hands are often as effectively tied—by Canon Law, their bishops, or by their pastors (in the instance of zealous young curates)—as those of the laity. Moreover, many of the supposed lay-clerical tensions often turn out to be tensions of an entirely different order: conflict between liberals and conservatives, younger generation and older, liturgists and mariologists, pluralistic and ghetto Catholics. Nevertheless, despite these important qualifications, it is inescapable that there is an imbalance between laity and clergy in the Church.

The net impact of this imbalance, while innocuous enough in earlier centuries, has been, in our time, to bring about an increasingly delicate situation. Given the present status of the laity in the Church, it is exceedingly difficult to see how, in fact, lay aspirations can be realized. It is not less difficult to see how clerical aspirations for a more effective, integrated laity can be realized either. Without some fundamental canonical changes and theological development the most that can be hoped for would be slow, halting, and probably meager improvements. As things stand now, lay aspiration is for the most part in direct conflict with possibility.

What aggravates this conflict, making it significantly different from similar ones in other eras, is that both education and clerical exhortation have led the layman to set very high goals. It is hardly too much to say that many of the clergy have goaded the laity into expecting and asking for very much from the Church. The laity have done their own part in raising their sights but, on the whole, it is the theologians—indeed, popes and bishops—who have taken the lead in pressing for a fuller participation of the laity in the Church.

The dangerous part of the conflict between aspiration and possibility lies in the fact that laymen are increasingly being led to expect to play a role which the Church is in no position to let them play. The layman has been incited by the Church to ask for, and anticipate, a freedom and responsibility which, in the end, the contemporary Church is hardly prone to give him. Just as aspiration conflicts with possibility, so too expectation conflicts with probability. Nothing good can come from conflicts of this sort; on the contrary, considerable harm seems an inevitable result.

One obvious result could be anti-clericalism. If the clergy leads the laity to expect changes which it is, in the end, prevented from bringing about (or unwilling in practice to bring about) much good will between laity and clergy is bound to be lost. The clergy will then have done little more than help to create a profoundly frustrated, disenchanted laity. The whole trend in recent decades has been (in theory mainly) toward greater responsibility for the laity: if this responsibility is not in fact given, the results will be far worse than if there had been no movement in the first place.

A reaction has already, to some extent, begun to set in. It can be seen, if the signs will be read, in the unwillingness of many recent Catholic college graduates to join parish or Church organizations; in the flight from Catholic higher education of many young Catholic scholars; in the transference of the zeal of many apostolic Catholics from Church to secular organizations; in the desire of innumerable Catholics to detach themselves from any cultural attachment to the Church, to lose themselves in a sheltering, pluralistic society.

The one distinctive thing that is likely to characterize this anti-clericalism—though a-clericalism might be a more precise term—is that it will be the product of thwarted dreams, frustrated hopes, and confounded apostolic zeal. But anti-clericalism is only the worst side of the picture; at the very least, the whole lay apostolate could simply wither away to a feeble, insignificant movement, of little consequence to the ongoing life of the Church. The only possibility for a genuinely effective lay apostolate is a clergy willing and *able* to give laymen both the freedom and respect—and independence—in non-dogmatic matters, needed to make the apostolate viable and attractive.

There is still another dimension to the lay-clerical relationship. One of the great and persistent problems of the Church is to keep popular piety consistent with theological developments. The traditional lag between the work of the theologians and the religious opinions of the people, while somewhat supportable in the past, cannot be afforded today. The liturgical movement, the social teachings of the Church, catechetics, and the Biblical revival have all suffered from this lag. Important and necessary advances have frequently suffered the fate of lay indifference or even hostility. A laity closely attuned to new developments, a laity working harmoniously with the clergy could help provide the kind of popular response to change lacking in the past.

The picture I have painted so far may seem unrelievedly dark, the possibilities of genuine progress slight. Given only the present structure of the Church, and given only the imbalance between lay aspirations and ecclesiastical reality, there would be little to justify much optimism. Fortunately, there is much more to be said. There is, despite its limitations, the unprecedented establishment of the preparatory commission of the lay apostolate; there is the work of many theologians on the theological problem of the laity, there is the increasing (if not dramatic) reliance of many bishops and priests on lay assistance. There is, most importantly, the undoubted loyalty of the laity to the Church.

The one thing that saves the American Church from classical anti-clericalism is that lay desires are not based on ideals counter to those of the Church; they stem from ideals thoroughly Catholic in origin and content. They stem from ideals held by the Church and affirmed by the Church—but which are not put into practice. The great danger is not loss of faith. The great danger is that of a loss of hope and interest, a loss of zeal and idealism. This would be a grievious loss to the Church, a grievious spiritual loss to those laymen who have staked so much on the future of the lay movement.

Here lies the importance of the Second Vatican Council. It is within the power of the Council to bring about effective reforms, to make those changes which will give both clergy and laity wider scope of action and greater self-responsibility. It can, if it will, do even more: it could, conceivably, give the layman some consultative role in the magisterium itself. There are both historical precedents and common sense reasons to support some move in this direction. The only real hope for an effective, engaged, active laity is that, by some means, they be given a hearing on those hierarchical decisions which intimately concern them, a hearing on those matters which bear directly on their needs, capacities, and talents. The great challenge of the Council is to find means to bring this goal about without sacrificing that necessary authority which must remain in the hands of the hierarchy and clergy.

There is no reason why a trained, loyal, integrated laity should in any respect pose a threat to the authority of the Church or its divinely ordained means of teaching and preserving the deposit of faith. There is, even more, no sound reason to assume that the laity would abuse any greater freedom given them. It ought to be within the genius of the Church to find ways of preserving the authority and office of the clergy while at the same time increasing the freedom and self-responsibility of the laity.

The desire of the laity today is only that the clergy engage in some careful soul-searching; that the Council give its utmost attention not only to a more effective utilization of the laity in the Church's mission to the world but also to the needs of the laity with respect to the inner life of the Church. To even face the problems and needs suggested here, much less to find solutions to them, will require much boldness. But it is a boldness not impossible for the Church.

CHAPTER FOUR

Confronting Protestantism

O NE THING COMMON TO DISCUSSION BETWEEN PROTESTANTS AND
Catholics is that each will at some point feel that he is misunderstood by the other. Part of this is attributable to the difficulties that beset any attempt to communicate one's most deeply
rooted allegiances, and part to the very human unwillingness to
believe that someone could really understand us and yet not be
convinced. The possibility of mutual understanding between the
Catholic and the Protestant arises only when each begins to wonder
if he fully grasps what the other is saying, however much he may
be convinced that he already knows. Equally important, a certain
amount of skepticism concerning the standard reasons given for
misunderstanding—bigotry, pride, lack of knowledge—can be a
healthy symptom of progress even though one's skepticism may
turn out to be unfounded.

As often as not, to be sure, mutual understanding will only serve to sharpen differences, to dash hopes and solidify divisions. Understanding can be a sword that cuts two ways; it may lessen personal antagonism and increase ideological antagonism.

Something like this is happening in the current attempts of a number of Catholics to gain new insights into Protestantism, both in its historical and in its contemporary manifestations. Not only has one result been to reveal that the theological gap between Protestantism and Catholicism has widened since the Reformation but, as Christopher Dawson has suggested, that there is an equally wide cultural division which has contributed to the separation.

There have, of course, been signs here and there of late that Catholic liturgy and ecclesiology are receiving greater attention from Protestants, just as there has been a growing awareness among Catholics that Protestantism can contribute something to Catholicism. Encouraging as this development might be, however, it is hard to dispute the judgment of Father Gustave Weigel, S.J., who, in *Faith and Understanding in America* (Macmillan, 1959), says, "Thanks to the ecumenical movement, many Protestants are tentatively formulating a concept of the Church which timorously approaches the Catholic notion; but in the rest of the articles we are worlds apart. In spite of the efforts of the neosupernaturalists who stress the transcendence of God, many Protestants, clerical and lay, theological and nontheological, identify God with something in man."

This is a hard saying and not, I would guess, the sort of quotation which many Catholics and Protestants interested in reunion like to see a Catholic emphasizing as I have chosen to do here. But if it is not the kind of judgment that augurs well for the future, it is still the fruit of an attempt to understand by a theologian who is anything but truculently gleeful over his own conclusions. While it may look like the sort of judgment Catholics have been levelling at Protestants ever since the Reformation, the main difference is that now Catholics look upon Protestantism as something other than a false system to be refuted and repudiated out of hand.

It is not Catholicism that suffers from Christian disunity, nor is it Protestantism as such, but all of us, Catholic and Protestant, bear to some extent a mutual guilt and share in the scandal of antagonism and separation. Just who is the *most* guilty is a matter for theologians to dispute—conceivably there could be a bit of wrangling on that point—and it would perhaps be silly to ask theologians to give up this sort of dispute for the sake of, say, a greater common strength against television and Sunday morning golf. What is important is that the results of the attempts to comprehend be used, not as ammunition to be stored in an apologetical armory, but simply as the data with which both sides must work.

The significance of the renewed Catholic interest in Protestantism is not, I would guess, that Catholics are more tolerant theologically of Protestants (which is hardly true) or that Catholics are only now coming to see the evil of disunity. Rather, it is that the Olympian manner, the scornful detachment, is giving way to a desire to meet Protestants in the flesh, to, if you will, grapple with men like ourselves over things that concern us both. Undoubtedly, those who see this trend as indicative of a need for greater unity against the common enemy of Communism and secularism have a plausible point, but I am inclined to agree with Mr. Dawson that the rise of the pluralistic society has done more than anything else to soften, if not destroy, the purely human and cultural barriers that have impeded reconciliation.

To the tough-minded, those who are concerned only with issues and not men, this change may appear an irrelevant matter. From the Catholic who looks only for submission, the more abject the better, and the Protestant who looks only for Rome to give up its pretensions, especially the extravagances of the First Vatican Council, little can be expected. It is not that what such men want is illogical or uncharitable. For the Catholic at least, there can be no objection to Father Weigel's statement, "While the mathematician is not obliged in logic to make all men mathematicians, the Catholic actually must desire that every human being become a Catholic." Instead, the difficulty with the tact of the tough-minded is that it is so hopelessly implausible to think that each side would ever give way *en masse* to such surrender terms.

The difference in the tenor of the Catholic approach today is that what was once thrown out as a demand is now looked upon as an ideal, even though there is a substantial segment of Catholicism which still adheres to the, should we say, hydrogen bomb way of scoring a point. This shift from demanding to hoping is no less logical and consistent but shows that the ideal is shot through with a greater respect for the providential ways of God and a more delicate sensitivity to the actual contingencies of the non-Catholic Christian and the demands made upon his integrity by his cultural and existential situation.

It is not a mistake to hope for conversion, for the committed believer can hardly do otherwise if his commitment purports to have any universal meaning and value. The real question is the way one chooses to express one's hopes. If they are given substance with a bludgeon, by verbal bullying, denunciations and slick refutations of formal errors, then they will be rejected and resented, whatever their validity, because, to use a Quaker expression, they will not "speak to the condition" of the hearer. Joseph Conrad, in *Under Western Eyes,* expressed perfectly the difficulties inherent in any attempt to use logic as the exclusive tool of analysis and criticism: "A train of thought is never false. The falsehood lies deep in the necessities of existence, in secret fears and half-formed ambitions, in the secret confidence combined with a secret mistrust of ourselves, in the love of hope and the dread of uncertain days." Father Weigel expresses a kindred idea when he says, "All religions have this in common, that they move the will through the excitation of an inward vision." And the trouble with trying to confute inward visions is that only the beholder can see clearly wherein their motive force lies; the blind outsider almost always misses the point.

The most one can do is to attempt to enable the other to catch a glimpse of one's own vision, to purify oneself so that what is essential comes through. Father George Tavard, A.A., in *The Church, The Layman and the Modern World* (Macmillan, 1959), exhorts us to do just this through our life as Catholics in the community and in the parish. Should we secretly be prone to think that the task of the Catholic is simply to present a better set of arguments, Father Tavard reminds us: "That there are genuine Christians who deny the Church is made possible by the necessary ambiguities affecting all realities that participate in the events of history. The faults and failures of the men who are in the Church, their twofold engagement in faith and in secular activities, their occasional insincerity, throw shadows on the garments of the Church. Because of them she is more or less hidden behind a haze of equivocation."

If giving witness to the truth of Catholicism is the essential task of the Catholic, it is no simple matter to know how to give the right kind of witness. Despite what many have said, particularly in decrying a lack of radicalism and boldness in today's younger generation, there is some reason to think that the problem of modern man is not that there are no powerful ideas or movements to capture his imagination. If anything there are too many, and the pull of each offering him the absolute solution to all his problems tends to leave him jaded of the whole business of seeking and embracing absolutes. Too many movements and ideologies have in recent years betrayed their followers and their ideals. If this has been a salutary lesson in the political realm, the extension of the lesson to cover religion is not surprising. Catholicism cannot fail to be suspect just because it does offer some absolute answers to the most fundamental human questions.

As Father Tavard notes, it is the false identification of Catholicism with the totalitarian mentality which is one of the main stumbling blocks of non-Catholics. Quite correctly he says, "One sees well enough the core of Blanshard's arguments: the Church claims the total spiritual allegiance of her members; by thus depriving them of man's right to his private judgment (as seen by Blanshard) she encourages a blind obedience which is likely to accept totalitarian politics." Far from always drawing men by its exalted vision, its inner consistency, and its tight logic, it is the very strength of Catholicism which makes it seem the most deadly kind of temptation for one determined to stand by himself and to exert to the fullest the most precious gift of freedom.

There can be no doubt that Protestantism has always been disturbed by the proliferation of sects entailed by its systematic rejection of a central, visible authority, and has been just as disturbed by the distortion of Christianity often justified in the name of freedom and progress. But while these facts have, to the Catholic, been the observable evidence of the fatal weakness of Protestantism, the Protestant himself has felt his choice to lie between the danger of error and the danger of spiritual tyranny. His choice of the former as the lesser evil is, to him, more consistent with the exercise of Christian liberty, no matter how much certainty and stability the latter might offer.

For the Catholic, perhaps, these choices as seen by the Protestants represent a false dilemma: divinely appointed authority is the very opposite of tyranny and certainly in fundamentals does not impair freedom but is the very ground of it. Yet it is difficult for the Catholic to make this sort of distinction persuasively in a world which exhibits innumerable great and petty authoritarian regimes, each suppressing the individual in the name of some greater good or truth. The very subtlety of Catholic reasoning on the meaning of Christian freedom is suspect; the impossibility of reducing the Catholic conception to a slogan suitable for a banner or placard only increases the suspicion that nothing more than devious reasoning lies behind it. Political and ideological totalitarianism have wreaked tremendous human suffering in our times; they have also debased language to such an extent that many of the words and concepts necessary for Catholics to make themselves understandable—"authority," "discipline," and "truth" for instance—are only understood according to the distorted usage of the dictator.

Inevitably, in this kind of situation, the Church will be misunderstood, even by those inclined to give it every benefit of the doubt. Because its view of the world is, up to a point, fixed and closed, rigidity will be read into it where none exists. That the Church is admittedly authoritarian, again up to a point, means that authoritarianism will be read into it in areas where the Catholic is perfectly free to choose for himself. Indeed, for the outsider the

matter of Catholic freedom must be baffling when he contem-
plates the frequently violent debates within the Church over the
degree of freedom allowable when a particular doctrine or practice
is in question. That the non-Catholic should, because it accords
with his preconceptions, choose that party in a dispute as most
representative which lessens the degree of freedom, ought not to
shock the Catholic who may at times find himself in a quandary
when faced with conflicting theological judgments. Moreover,
the traditional language of Catholicism is not the language of the
day and, as Father Weigel points out, the Catholic who attempts
to translate the traditional language into a contemporary idiom
may satisfy neither the outsider nor his fellow Catholics. It is all
too easy for the non-Catholic to disregard the persuasive and con-
genial Catholic as the exception proving the rule, particularly
when some Catholics themselves pass the same judgment.

If, for some of the above reasons, it is exceedingly difficult
for the Protestant to understand Catholicism, it is equally difficult for the Catholic to understand Protestantism. The Catholic will inevitably be prone to abstract some kind of essence of
Protestantism, perhaps as Father Weigel does by emphasizing its
conception of truth as a "construction" rather than a "reception."
At most, however, such abstractions will only be tentative guides,
as I'm sure Father Weigel himself would say.

At one time it may have been possible to generalize about
Protestantism. Today such generalizations are risky because of the
existence of a plethora of conflicting trends, ranging from those
who see Christianity as a useful myth when suitably interpreted
through those Anglicans who find the Bishop of Rome distress-
ingly low church. One can, as Fathers Weigel and Tavard have
done very effectively and convincingly, delineate trends within
Protestantism. But one can rarely be sure, given any individual
Protestant, where he personally will stand in relation to these
trends or even, as far as that goes, where he will stand in relation
to the creed of his own church.

While a Protestant would be justified in simply reading the
works of the great classical expositors of Catholicism with consid-

erable assurance that the contemporary Catholic would be one with them on fundamentals, a similar approach by Catholics to Protestantism would not equally be justified. The Catholic can only confront the Protestant one by one; his dialogue cannot be with spokesmen for an institution, for there are no such spokesmen nor is there any such institution.

The Protestant is justified in looking not for the eccentric witness to Catholicism but for the corporate witness. The Catholic may be tempted to look at Protestantism in the same way and, to some extent, this is reasonable enough. Yet if to the Protestant the glory of his faith is that it gives the individual a radical freedom to probe the depths of Christianity for himself then, in all justice, it is the individual Protestant who must be met.

In time, it might be that Protestants and Catholics will come to understand each other. Should this ever happen, there would be, of course, no guarantee that anything at all would be changed in their relationship. A belief that understanding would make a difference is little more of a leap of faith—the only leap available to us.

PART II

Wrestling with the Secular

CHAPTER FIVE

The Legacy of Pio Nono

THE ELECTION OF A POPE IS ALWAYS A RISKY BUSINESS. TO PRE-
dict the direction and tone of his pontificate is more risky
still. When Giovanni Mastai-Ferretti, a relatively obscure Cardinal from Imola, just south of Bologna, was elected Pope Pius IX
in 1846, there was considerable rejoicing. The word was out that
providentially, against all odds, the new pope was a progressive.
Wasn't it true, gossip had it, that he wanted to illuminate the dark
streets of Rome with gas? Wasn't he known to be intrigued with
railroads and scientific methods of agriculture? After Pope Gregory
XVI, austere in his ways, violently opposed to the "modern liberties," any pope would be an improvement. But to get a genuine
liberal, one of whose first acts was to free a thousand political
prisoners, was almost beyond belief. A new day had clearly arrived
for the Church, and for months the new pope was the toast of

Europe. "A capital fellow," exclaimed one Oxford don. Viva Pio
Nono! was the cry.

The enthusiasm was a trifle misplaced. Before he died, some
thirty-two years later, the name of Pius IX had become synon-
ymous with everything the contemporary world distrusted in the
Church: the denial of religious liberty, Roman authoritarianism,
papal pretensions, and a cocksure, imperialistic theology. This was
fine for some. Cardinal Manning, in a burst of enthusiasm, wrote
that "When the history of the Pontificate of Pius IX shall be
written, it will be found to have been one of the most resplendent, majestic, and powerful." For others, the "resplendent"
pontificate was in reality a disaster. Montalembert, his patience at
an end, would ask indignantly in 1870: "Who could have led us to
foresee in 1847 . . . the permanent triumph of those lay theologians of absolutism who have begun by making a sacrifice of all
our liberties, of all our principles, of all our earlier ideas . . . in
order, in due course, to offer up justice and truth, reason and history, as a holocaust to the idol which they are erecting at the
Vatican?"

Whatever the ultimate judgment of history, Montalembert
appears to have had good reasons for his anger. It was he, after all,
who for decades had sought to bring about a meeting of minds
between the Church and the new order which swept Europe in
the nineteenth century. Pio Nono set his face against this order,
and in the end came to judge Montalembert a proud, angry, rash,
and violent man. So he was, in many ways, but history was on his
side. When the final session of Vatican II ended in December of
1965, the mind of the fathers was clear: there must be an end to
Catholic ambiguity on religious liberty; there must be an end to
that conception of the Church which sees the papacy as its ultimate meaning; there must be an end to extravagant mariology,
intent upon piling up one title after another in Mary's name.

In short, Vatican II can well be looked upon as an effort to
undercut, and thus correct, the three most prominent notes of
Pio Nono's reign. For it was Pio Nono who most decisively cast
the mold for the Church's suspicion of religious liberty; who set in

motion the development of Marian doctrines; and who presided over that Council which defined the infallibility of the pope, an act which led directly to papal centralization and authoritarianism. The centenary of the *Syllabus of Errors* was noted in December of 1964. It was not celebrated.

What is the meaning of this decisive shift? What does it tell us about the Church? How could Pio Nono have failed so decisively to gauge the temper of the coming world? These questions are not easy to answer, and it is terribly easy to oversimplify history in trying to get at them. But it is worth the effort. The Church has still not learned to live with the modern world. True, it has come to see that the way mapped out by Pius IX leads to a dead end; but that is hardly the same as finding a better way. That discovery has yet to be made.

It is almost an axiom today that to understand a man, a movement, or an idea, one has to know the historical context of the times. The axiom serves well in the case of Pio Nono. When he was born, on May 13, 1792, the French Revolution was well under way. The patience of the reigning Pope, Pius VI, had not at that point quite given way. But it was only a matter of time. The Civil Constitution of the Clergy, voted by the Constituent Assembly in 1790, had rapidly divided the French Church; those who refused to swear an oath to the Constitution faced the prospect of deportation, exile, and sometimes death. Whatever small authority Rome had managed to retain over the French church was all but nullified. The church became little more than a department of government. Even those priests who took the oath were soon hounded and persecuted. The Old Regime was at an end. In place of a romantic notion of the solidarity of Throne and Altar, liberty, fraternity and equality won the day—born, of course, to the cries of many bloody victims. Pius VI finally spoke out against the Revolution, and it would be many decades before a pope would have a good word to say for liberty.

For a time, Italy was free of strife. The Italian states, particularly those belonging to the papacy, seemed relatively secure. But by 1830 all of Europe was breaking up. The Belgian revolution of that year was quickly followed by revolts in the German and Italian states. In the latter instance, the secret society of the Carbonari aimed to establish a new republican state, and this to the cost of the papal states. This was too much for Pius VI's successor, Pope Gregory XVI. Not only was the temporal sovereignty of the papacy being seriously threatened for the first time, but in its train came a whole host of ideas that appalled the pope. The bitter fruits of revolutionary freedom were now all too apparent, striking right at the papacy itself. In his inaugural encyclical *Mirari Vos* (1832), Gregory XVI lashed out in all directions. Speaking of "the deplorable evils that at present afflict the Church," he condemned, as the arch villain, "Indifferentism, i.e., the fatal opinion, spread abroad by the villainy of evil men, that the soul's eternal salvation can be obtained by any kind of profession of faith provided that morals conform to justice and probity. . . . From this poisoned source of Indifferentism flows the false and absurd maxim, or rather madness, that every individual should be given and guaranteed freedom of conscience, that most contagious of errors. . . . With this is connected the freedom of the press, the most fatal and execrable of errors. . . ." He was hardly more sympathetic to a separation of Church and State: "Let princes remember that power has been given them not only for the sake of governing the world but especially to help and defend the Church."

The first Catholic victim of this broadside was Felicité de Lamennais, for the encyclical was directed as much against him and his paper *L'Avenir* as against the revolutionaries themselves. He had the temerity to argue for a "free church in a free state"! There were other victims as well, Montalembert and Lacordaire, most notably. But the real victim, in the end, was the Church itself. Gregory XVI placed the first set of chains around the Church. It remained only for Pius IX to put on the final padlocks. Not until well into the twentieth century would some fresh winds start to blow, however ingenious the skills of John Courtney Murray in discerning signs of a break in the late nineteenth-century encyclicals of Leo XIII.

The most famous document of Pius IX's pontificate is of course the *Syllabus of Errors,* attached as a list of proscribed opinions to the encyclical *Quanta Cura.* The *Syllabus* never loses its fascination, and no document perhaps has ever been subjected to such an array of ingenious explanations and rationales. I have long played with the following hypothesis: if one wants to know what the Church will be proclaiming within a hundred years, find out what it is at present condemning; at least a third of the forbidden opinions will, within a century, be fashionable theological clichés, uttered by laymen and popes alike. Naturally, one can't be sure *which* "pernicious errors" (as nineteenth century popes were wont to express themselves) will be accepted; but that *some* will, seems beyond historical doubt. Consider Proposition 80 of the *Syllabus,* the most famous of all. Condemned was the notion that "The Roman Pontiff can and should reconcile himself to any compromise with progress, liberalism and modern civilization." Or Proposition 77, equally reprobate: "In our age there is no longer any point in regarding the Catholic religion as the one state religion to the exclusion of all other forms of worship." That is enough; it is too painful and embarrassing to quote any more.

Even more embarrassing at this point in history is to recount the ingenious ways in which the sting was taken out of these propositions. Msgr. Dupanloup's explanation is the most celebrated, though he borrowed it from *Civiltá Cattolica:* the Pope was enunciating only the ideal, the "thesis." In practice, the Church was often quite willing to tolerate democratic ways, the separation of Church and state, freedom of speech and of the press. That was the "hypothesis." The distinction was not deceitful. There is solid evidence that the Pope himself accepted it. But that such a device would not fail to arouse even further suspicions—with its rank air of expediency—seemed never to enter his mind. Then, too, it has been argued that not all of the proscribed propositions were accounted heresy; some were merely dangerous notions. Again the evidence is good to support this qualification. Unfortunately, it was exceedingly difficult at the time to tell which was which. Another argument, equally well founded, was that the Pope condemned only those concepts of liberty which sprang from a rationalistic, naturalistic view of man. The point is a valid one, weakened only by the fact that the Pope never undertook to explain how democratic liberty, under any circumstances, could be a positive political or spiritual good.

The crowning argument, however, is to grant that Pio Nono was excessive in his *anathemas*; to grant that he was harsh toward those Catholic liberals who sought a middle way; to grant that his understanding of the historical drive of revolutionary Europe was lacking in insight. But once having made these concessions, he is then defended all the more fervently. How could he have done otherwise, faced as he was with rampant anticlericalism and anti-religion? How could he have taken a lofty view of a revolutionary fervor which led directly to the murder of his good friend Count Pelligrino Rossi, himself a revolutionary? How could he be expected to defend a use of freedom whose first target was the Church itself? These questions are not easy to answer; more than one man, despite his best intentions, has been trapped by historical circumstances.

We had better not be so easily disarmed. If no more is expected from the Vicar of Christ than from any other man, one can easily accept these arguments. But what if we hold up a higher standard, the standard, say, which was bequeathed to us by the Council which Pius IX himself called? Formally taken, Vatican I did no more than define those very narrow conditions under which the Pope is said to speak infallibly. But to say that hardly exhausts the mystique of the papacy which Vatican I engendered. True enough, the Council fathers did not go as far as Manning, W. G. Ward, or Veuillot would have liked, but they went far enough to give the papacy a glory and claim which no other institution could match. Ever since that time, the papacy has evoked a sense of awe in the Church which few have dared challenge. Perhaps this is all wrong, a case of letting our reverence run ahead of our theology; nonetheless, that is what we were brought up on. To hold, on the one hand, that Pius IX was genuinely the Vicar of Christ, and thus protected in a special way by the Holy Spirit; and then to be forced to argue, on the other, that he was merely a victim of historical circumstance—well, one has to become fairly agile, to say the least.

And agile we became. At least three generations of Americans, for instance, had to learn a host of hairsplitting, tortured arguments to show that their dedication to the American Constitution was fully compatible with nineteenth-century papal pronouncements. For those Catholics who styled themselves political liberals, friends of human liberty, the obstacles were no less formidable. They had to explain that the term "liberal Catholic" was not a contradiction in terms, no easy task since the circle around Pius IX at the time of Vatican I had succeeded in making it a catch-all phrase for every manner of deviation and heterodoxy. (One strategy, a wise friend once told me, was to call oneself a "Catholic liberal" rather than a "liberal Catholic.")

Perhaps the matter should not be treated so lightly, even now. For the inevitable effect of all these strategies was really to harm the Catholic's devotion to the Holy See, though the intention was quite otherwise. In practice, they meant that one could never really listen to the Pope with an open spirit. The minute he spoke, calculations had to begin. Was this sentence binding? Was that sentence only a recommendation? The spiritual life had to be lived on two levels, the level of docility and the level of cunning exegesis, creative reading of impossible passages. How could one, at exactly the same moment, profess undying fidelity to the popes and yet deny that one was in any way bound to some perfectly clear instance of papal teaching? Yet that is exactly what Catholics living in pluralistic nations were forced to do when confronted with the texts of Pius IX on religious liberty. The only way out was to become one of Jules Feiffer's "explainers"; the explanations are valid enough, but there eventually comes a point at which the spirit dies, smothered to death by distinctions, qualifications and choking loopholes. The successful drive for a strong statement on religious liberty at Vatican II can be seen as much as an attempt to escape this dank atmosphere in the Church as a desire to recognize the non-Catholic conscience. The world learned to live with a Church which equivocates on freedom of conscience; it could probably go on doing so. It is really the Catholic himself who can't stand it any more.

Oddly enough, the least controversial of Pio Nono's many proclamations was his definition of the doctrine of the Immaculate Conception of the Blessed Virgin on December 8, 1854. Odd at least to us today, living in a time when Marian devotions have lost much of their drive. But it was not so during the nineteenth century for that was the century of Marian apparitions, of Catherine Labouré and Bernadette Soubirous, of Pauline Jaricot's "living rosary," the apparition at La Salette; and the century as well which saw a new burst of enthusiasm for eucharistic devotions, indulgences, veneration of relics, and elaborate pilgrimages. Many there were who saw in the Marian apparitions a special grace from God to help counter the rationalism and scientism of the era. Be that as it may, the special devotion of Pius IX to the Virgin was easily equalled by popular piety. From France especially there came many requests for a definition of the doctrine of the Immaculate Conception. Of some six hundred replies to a request from the Pope to the bishops for prayer and advice on the question, only two or three felt that the doctrine was not definable; only a few more felt that a formal definition would be inopportune. The difficulties which had, long before, been expressed by St. Bernard and St. Thomas Aquinas were quickly swept aside. The lack of a direct scriptural foundation for the doctrine posed no greater difficulty, and was more than balanced by a long liturgical tradition and the common belief of the faithful. The matter might not have gone so easily in the middle of the twentieth century, but the solemn definition of the doctrine in the middle of the nineteenth was met with general rejoicing. Only in isolated German theological groups was the enthusiasm a good deal more restrained.

Significantly enough, the very manner of the proclamation of the doctrine was an augury of the direction the papacy was taking. Despite the overwhelming support of the bishops for the definition, the Pope deliberately chose to issue it in his name alone, going so far as to formally reject a request from two bishops that the text of the proclamation mention the fact of episcopal approval. While there can be no doubt that the Pope carefully solicited episcopal opinion before acting, it was no less true, as one of Pio Nono's principal biographers, Roger Aubert, has put it, "that the final act, at which the bishops assisted as simple spectators, placed in singular relief the person of the Pope." Thus was set a precedent of far-reaching consequences, effectively laying the ground for the definition of papal infallibility. When the fathers of Vatican II wrote in the third chapter of the *Constitution on the Church*, that the definitions of a pope "of themselves, and not from the consent of the Church, are justly styled irreformable . . . and therefore they need no approval of others, nor do they allow an appeal to any other judgment," they were only echoing Vatican I. More than any other pope, then, Pio Nono effectively limited the importance of the episcopal college. Every pope since then has done as he did: diligently soliciting the views of the bishops and then, at the final moment acting independently and with patent sovereignty. Despite the efforts of the fathers at Vatican II, it remains difficult to see that the principle of "collegiality" has gone appreciably beyond the line drawn by Pius IX.

It might have been otherwise in the nineteenth century but for a paradoxical combination of trends and events. This combination can be summed up in one word: ultramontanism. In its early phases, ultramontanism came to life as part of a growing conviction that the only way the Church could get out from under the yoke of the state was by a closer attachment to the papacy. If Count Joseph De Maistre can be called the father of ultramontanism, he could count some odd children in his family. One of these was the same Felicité de Lamennais who was all but read out of the Church by one of those popes he was trying to bring into a new prominence. De Maistre and Lamennais could hardly have had less in common, the former an ardent royalist, the latter an equally ardent advocate of the people. But they both saw how the subservience of the Church to the state prior to the French Revolution had seriously weakened its spiritual influence and independence. De Maistre wanted a free Church, but a Church which worked hand in hand with a respectful monarchical state. For his part, Lamennais saw prophetically that only a radical break with the entire tradition of Church-State alliance could give both the Church and the people their just liberty. For each, however, a strong papacy was an absolute prerequisite. Somehow or other, the Pope would once again have to become the effective center of the Church universal.

As the century progressed, however, the initial ultramontane drive for a strong papacy gradually came to take the form of a vigorous drive for a definition on papal infallibility. How better, many felt, could the Church establish once and for all the Pope's spiritual power than to declare him incapable of error in matters of faith and morals? What the Church had lost during the century in temporal prestige it could more than regain in spiritual stature! There was an attractive symmetry in this politico-theological equation, and it was to prove irresistible. With every reverse the Church secular suffered, the pressure for a mighty triumph by the Church spiritual was intensified. And so it turned out, despite the efforts of a few to stem the ultramontane tide (especially Acton, Döllinger, and Newman). Within the space of less than forty years, what had begun as an avant garde movement ended as a symbol of conservative intransigence.

Just how active a part Pius IX took in behalf of the definition of infallibility at the Council remains a matter of debate. That he favored the definition is beyond dispute; whether he improperly manipulated the Council to insure it is another matter. Suffice it to say that he openly sided with the Ultramontane party, occasionally impugned the motives of the liberal minority, and welcomed the efforts of the majority leaders to introduce the topic of infallibility early in the Council and out of turn. At most, his conduct was something less than seemly for one so intimately affected by the conciliar debate; but that is probably all that can, in justice, be said.

Pio Nono died on February 7, 1878. At his side was Cardinal Manning, his long-time friend and companion. It was not, in one way, a happy time to die. Despite the efforts of a lifetime to stem the tides of hostility toward the Church, to shore up its spiritual walls, there was little to show in the way of success. The hostility continued to grow, and right under the Pope's window as well. Three years after his death, while his body was being moved to its final resting place in the Church of San Lorenzo Fuori le Mura, the coffin was splattered with mud by a hostile Roman mob. The anticlericalism he fought against had the last say.

The judgment of the mob was too harsh. Pius IX was no villain. But he was, perhaps, someone even more dangerous. He was a man who used the wrong weapons at the wrong time to fight for the wrong cause. The weapons he picked were those of condemnation and bitter denunciation. The time he chose was that moment in Western history when the idea of human liberty was on the verge of becoming a reality. The cause he defended was that of the Church's worldly glory and secular standing. To the rising proletariat he had little to say. To those Catholics trying to find a theological base for the revolutionary freedoms, he offered only opposition. To the efforts of those few men who were seeking the Church's support for a vigorous program of social justice he was almost totally blind.

Does all of this mean he was a failure? That is my suspicion but it may not quite do. Let us say that he was a Catholic of his times, the leader of a Church doomed to be smashed by history. He did what any ordinary Catholic might have done: he fought. In the words of Macaulay "he confronted the tempest without flinching; and was faithful to the end." One can admire that in a pope. One can also wish he had lived in another century, one less crucial, less decisive. His virtues continue to be our burden. The Church he sought to fashion might well withstand the gates of hell. But it could not withstand the spirit of men seeking liberation. That liberation has not yet been achieved. Whether another pope, another generation of bishops, another generation of Catholics can help bring it about remains to be seen.

CHAPTER SIX

The New Pluralism

As WE ALL KNOW, THE ELECTION OF JOHN F. KENNEDY IN 1960 WAS taken as decisive evidence that the Catholic minority had "come of age" in America. It was also taken as proof that the fearful myth of "Catholic power" in Paul Blanshard's sense had been exploded, the purported "pluralism" of our society vindicated, and the way opened for a creative confrontation with the "Protestant-Catholic-Jew" image of American society which, according to Will Herberg, has come to supplant the old ethnic composition of our people. In brief, America seemed well on its way to becoming the promised land of pluralism in fact as well as theory.

There was surely something attractive in this reading of Mr. Kennedy's election; it had its elements of truth. It has also become hopelessly outdated. The real confrontation with pluralism is only now beginning. At most, Mr. Kennedy's election proved that a Catholic could be elected to the Presidency—if he went to Har-

46

vard, was a Democrat, had a rich father, a beautiful wife, a finely tuned political machine, and some plain good luck. I say this not by way of dismissing the changes which the election implied, but only to recall Catholic romanticists to their senses.

It was not Mr. Kennedy's good fortune which made pluralism a fact. That honor must go to the recent Supreme Court prayer and Bible-reading decisions. By and large, they were unpopular—it is difficult to imagine Congress or any state legislature voting for such decrees. Many people in fact, would now like to see a constitutional amendment which would reflect popular feeling and reinstate "our religious heritage." In the sense that the decisions were unpopular, it can be said that they were not genuinely pluralistic. To judge from the laments, they violated the sensibilities of the "majority." This is an intelligible, if not fully persuasive argument.

The real curiosity that emerges from the decisions lies in the variety of responses which they elicited. Jews on the whole welcomed them—no surprise there. Protestants reacted with mixed feelings—that was a little suprising; one might have expected more opposition. But that Catholics should, with near unanimity on the first decision and vigorous if less heated objections on the second, be the most prominent dissenters is remarkable. Who would have supposed beforehand that Catholics would have become indignant when prayers were taken out of what they have often called the "Godless public schools"? True, that is a bad joke and one which does violence to the good intentions and religious zeal of the Catholic critics. Put with more delicacy, who would have supposed that Catholics would take the lead in defending an American "religious heritage" the roots of which are Protestant and deist and which, until very recently, was hardly more than a quasi-establishment of Protestantism?

There are many possible answers to these questions. One I would like to propose is this: Catholics have willingly and even vociferously defended the American separation of Church and State because they have been able to enjoy the next best thing, a close bond between religion (writ large) and American culture.

The short of the matter is that America has been a religious, indeed, a quasi-sacral society; hence, in sacrificing any desire for a union of Church and State, only the icing of the religio-pluralistic cake has been omitted. What need is there for a formal partnership of cleric and legislator when the forces of tradition, custom, and social conformity guarantee that religion will remain a dominant force in society?

To say this is not to cast any doubt, even indirectly, on the American Catholic dedication to the separation of Church and State. It is rather to assert that the recent Court decisions have shown that there still remain in the bones of the Catholic strong traces of his ancestral dependence upon a sacral society to shore up, promote, and honor religious values. One might even go so far as to suggest that there has been an unacknowledged proviso in Catholic enthusiasm for the separation of Church and State: such a separation is good so long as it does not jeopardize a favored place for religious values in our cultural, political, and juridical life. Put another way, Church and State may be separate as long as this does not disturb the ancient premise which was once thought to entail their close union: that the State has an obligation to cooperate with, and give public support and comfort to religion. The Catholic reaction against the decisions could thus be explained as an awareness that now the premise itself is being called into question.

The Supreme Court decisions have cast starkly before Catholics the fact that America is ceasing to be a religio-sacral society with the Christian religion riding in the seat of power. Whatever one may think of the decisions, they were inevitable. In the largest sense they confirmed what by now ought to be obvious, that there exists in this country a large Jewish-secular minority (supported by many Protestants) who are not committed to the American religious heritage in the form in which it developed over the course of American history. Why should they be so committed, especially when experience has taught them that this tradition imposes many burdens on their conscience? Do they not have the right, as much as the Christian, to make their values count in our society?

Why should they be forced to conform to majority values (or accept concessions from that majority), as if, somehow, American values were fixed once and for all before their arrival and need not now be adapted to the changes which their presence would suggest? As it happened, it took the Supreme Court to make their voices count; but sooner or later the legislative process would have achieved the same effect.

How hard it seems for Catholics to accept this change. Why? I have already suggested one reason: that Catholics are far less willing to relinquish the old idea of a sacral society than even they themselves recognize. Despite all the disputes with Protestants over the years, Catholics have profited from the fact that religion and Christianity have been favored and abetted. There is still another and more disturbing reason. In spite of the incessant discussion among Catholics over the last two decades about "Catholicism and pluralism," it is now apparent that it touched only one part of the problem: the gaining of a place for Catholics comparable to their number and the overcoming of those disabilities imposed upon them by the dominant (Protestant) majority. Much of this discussion was defensive in its thrust: the answering of attacks, the allaying of suspicions and, internally, the theological struggle to convince other Catholics (in Rome and at home) that the American system was favorable to Catholicism. It is that discussion which Mr. Kennedy's election served in great part to halt.

But it did little to prepare the ground for the new shape of American pluralism, a pluralism which must now take account of a new minority, one whose disabilities in the past were as great if not greater than any borne by Catholics. The question today is not: Is Catholicism compatible with American democratic pluralism set within a Christian context (the old situation)? Instead, Is Catholicism compatible with the new pluralism, set now within a context in which, step by step, religion is losing its traditional privileges, in which it has steadily to give way to the pressures and demands of those opposed to any form (even cultural) of a sacral society? In the past, America had a "neutral" state—favorable to religion. We now have a state which is becoming truly neutral—favorable neither to belief nor unbelief. That so many Catholics have desperately begun claiming that the emergent "neutrality" actually favors unbelief is, I fear, indicative of dependence upon the old sacralism.

It is not possible to say the same thing about the Jewish community or of an important segment of Protestant thought. The reasons for the different responses to the changing pluralism are well brought out in a valuable book by Rabbi Arthur Hertzberg, Martin Marty, and Monsignor Joseph Moody, *The Outbursts that Await Us* (Macmillan, 1964), subtitled "Three Essays on Religion and Culture in America."

Rabbi Hertzberg expresses very directly the underlying reason why most Jews support the prayer decisions. "In the hard school of suffering Jews have learned to feel almost instinctively that their freedom is safest—indeed that they can even achieve freedom—only in societies in which the church is blunted in its dominance of public life." In addition, "the rise of the modern secular state was the *sine qua non* to the political emancipation of the Jews." Though all Jews would not accept Rabbi Hertzberg's analysis, the majority probably would. Thus, it is easy to see why the Court decisions were greeted as a special kind of emancipation for the Jews: no longer would they have to accept a whole range of religious practices in the public schools which reminded them of the Christian hegemony in American life. Yet as Rabbi Hertzberg also adds (somewhat ambiguously), "The First Amendment is not the real dogma of the American Jew. His deepest and most messianic need is not a completely secular state; *it is a truly equal status in American culture.*" The fact—and a sad one it is—that so many Catholics seem totally unable to comprehend how a believing Jew could actually want religion removed from public life bespeaks both a misunderstanding of the Jews and an almost constitutional inability to conceive of a society of religious men who do not want some kind of favor from the State.

This latter viewpoint, however, is one which a new generation of Protestant thinkers finds comprehensible. In his essay, Martin Marty graphically sketches a new direction for American Protestantism. "If there is," he writes, "a potential in secularity and validity to pluralism and if the Christian has nothing to fear in exposing his truth to other truths, then his truth calls him to that exposure." The critical phrase here is "a potential in secularity and validity to pluralism." Dr. Marty is willing to affirm what so many Christians seem unwilling to accept: that secularity could be a positive good—not only for the State, but for society as well. "Somehow one senses," he says, "long after the official end of the age of Constantine, a real fear among Christians including Protestants that the faith cannot persist without the shelter of an official culture, without the pretext of quasi-legal props." "More and more," he writes in another place, "the churches seem to want the pluralistic society to do what they fail to do individually and ecclesiastically. They want it to be productive of values, want it to be the teacher."

All of this is apt to be misunderstood. Dr. Marty is not calling on Protestants for a harmless, inoffensive Christianity which refuses to make its voice heard in the market place. On the contrary, he asks only for a "postimperial view of Protestantism. . . . That is, a self-critical Protestantism which does not rely on a Protestant culture, [one which] must be more disciplined, more informed, more sacrificial and thus—in Christian terms—more productive than the self-enhancing form which wants laws and culture and ethos to do its work for it." But it is not Protestantism alone, I would add, which harbors these attitudes. If Catholicism has never had an "imperial" era in America, it has often sought to have "laws and culture and ethos do its work for it." Catholics as well as Protestants still show the heritage of the Constantinian-Justinian settlements. Those settlements, Dr. Marty argues, "built into the Christian *psyche* that attitude toward the state which is still reflected in every request for exemptions and favors for religion."

There is, happily, little suggestion of such an attitude in Monsignor Moody's essay. He wisely points out that American pluralism was a product of circumstances and "practical necessity was its dynamic." His suggestion that "religion's most decisive social contribution is its effort to limit man's aggressiveness through love of God and neighbor," strikes me as a particularly valuable insight. More concretely, Monsignor Moody argues that "What religion can do is to strengthen belief in the democratic propositions by emphasizing their moral foundations," or, put another way, "to deepen the American political faith in democracy."

My uneasiness with Monsignor Moody's essay arises only when he observes that "American Catholics were the pioneers in adjusting to a pluralist society." In one obvious sense this is true. Catholics were for many decades the largest and most important minority group in a Protestant society. They fought the first battles and, by sheer force of number, had much to do with opening up our society to the influence of non-Protestants. But it is important not to forget that the pluralist society in question was a "Christian" society, and that the pioneering work involved the coexistence of Christians, not of believer and unbeliever. As matters stand today, Catholics are by no means acting like "pioneers" in facing the new shape of American pluralism. Instead, they are prone to be aligned with those Protestants, especially in the fundamentalist camp, who are disturbed that the good old days of religion are being cast aside in favor of what they choose to call "secularism." The pioneers have joined the rear guard.

But this objection is only a quibble, and a point worth mentioning because it serves to call attention to a comment by Monsignor Moody which I would hope could be taken with full seriousness by Catholics. "There is even a possibility," Monsignor Moody writes, "that American Catholics may have to learn, as have the Jews in so many areas, how to live in a society which does not reflect their values. This would be a new experience for them in America, for even in their earlier experience here the Protestant-dominated culture had values they could understand."

The question is, when should we begin to learn? Monsignor Moody does not believe that the problem is pressing: "I do not feel that Catholics will face this problem in the foreseeable future as religious feeling is still deeply imbedded in the people; were they to have to, I suspect that they would do it with the flexibility that their history in America suggests." Well, I am not at all confident that Catholics will respond with "flexibility." The reaction to the Court decisions was marked by rigidity, the hurling of charges, the retailing of the worst possible clichés. Doubtless there has been flexibility in the past; but signs of paralysis are everywhere in evidence.

Yet it is unlikely that the new pluralism will be given sufficent attention until Catholics begin thinking about the meaning of a "secular" society. This remark may seem surprising, for it can easily be pointed out that Catholic political thinkers and theologians have developed numerous delicate distinctions and rationales for full Catholic participation in pluralistic societies. The concept of the "state," for instance, is customarily distinguished from that of "society"; thus many thinkers can argue that it is improper to identify the duties of the state toward religion with those of society. Or again, it is common (following St. Thomas) to distinguish between good laws and good morality; hence the Catholic moralist will readily admit that not every immoral act should be prohibited by civil law. Such distinctions are useful. They have been the cornerstones upon which Catholics have based their claim to be full-hearted, democratic pluralistic Americans.

Nonetheless, their permanent utility may well be doubted, and this precisely because the *de facto* context in which these distinctions have been employed has been in a society steeped in Christian values. Even now it seems apparent that Catholic thought is ill-equipped to contribute any special creativity to a post-prayer-decision America—an America in which agnosticism has as much right to the full privileges of the state as does religion. A clue to this malaise lies in a certain either-or type of thinking common among Catholic thinkers: either the Courts must allow prayer in the public schools or the result will favor secularism; either religion must be aided in the public schools or a "religion of secularism" will be established; either our society must proclaim publicly its allegiance to God or it will become a God-less society; either religion must receive public recognition and privilege or we will have an agnostic, hedonistic citizenry. There is no sound reason to make such assumptions, to create such stark alternatives. They all stem from a poverty of imagination which, in effect, assumes that if religion is excluded from public support and special deference the result must inevitably favor the forces of anti-religion.

There are many possible explanations to account for a mentality which creates such black and white antitheses. The historical fact that many European attempts to strip religion of its privileges and protections were motivated by a rejection of religion itself cannot easily be forgotten. Nor is it difficult to find historical examples to show that a prime tactic of those opposed to religious values is to urge that religion be relegated to the private, personal, and subjective recesses of men's hearts, to remove it from the public order. But there is little evidence to suggest that anything of the kind is now taking place in America. On the contrary, a good case can be made that religious values now exercise, in some areas of our public life, a far greater influence than at any time in the past. (Whatever their failures in the past, the churches in America are now taking the lead, for instance, in the struggle against racial discrimination.) Those who have attacked, or litigated against, governmental support of religion have done so on the grounds that their rights were being infringed—not on the grounds that religious values are false or harmful values. Yet, somehow, Catholics find it hard to recognize this distinction.

The main reason, I would suggest, why many Catholics are prone to create antitheses is that they have never fully confronted the idea of a neutral state or of a secular society. Now that such a reality is beginning to emerge they are finding that the elaborate rationales of the past no longer work very efficiently—thus they fall back on what can only be called the clichés of nineteenth-century Catholicism: a secular state is necessarily a "secularistic" state, a neutral state is necessarily one inimical to religion, and so forth. The worst cliché of all is that if religion does not have a privileged place in society, then it must necessarily become only a private affair, with no force in the public arena.

The task which now lies before Catholics is to rid their mind of such vestiges of the past. Would not the children suffer if they never heard God mentioned or acknowledged in the public schools? Would not the citizens suffer if the lordship of God was not affirmed by the state? Would not the churches suffer if their special importance as moral and religious educators was not legislatively recognized? Would not the morals of citizens suffer if the state did not affirm the existence of an eternal, absolute code of conduct? All these things might indeed happen, but why should they? The only firm reason to suppose such a course of events is that religion is of its nature incapable of existing apart from state support and deference. Since no one is likely to accept such an idea (and history would quickly confute anyone who did), we are left with little more than speculation tinged with free-floating fear. In fact, in such a society as ours the churches and religion continue to have many important ways of educating the people and influencing public opinion on moral and religious matters, only one of which (and least important) is government support and special homage.

Equally important, there is much to be said for a genuinely secular (as opposed to secularistic) society, and much to support a Christain scrupulosity in asking nothing more from the state than freedom. The central question, then, is, how can we devise a society which is secular without being secularistic, a neutral state which does not favor unbelief, and a free society which does not work to the disadvantage of either religion or non-religion? Here, in essence, we have the great conundrum posed by the newly emergent American pluralism. It is a perplexity which will not be solved by pressing for a return to the good old days when, supposedly, America's "religious heritage" was accepted by all. And most surely it will not be solved as long as so many Christians assume that any limitation on the public homage to religion once offered by the American state amounts to the establishment of secularism.

There will be no painless or simple solution. The needs of the new pluralistic situation will require restraint from every one of the groupings of men who make up our society—from believers and unbelievers, Jews, Protestants and Catholics. As for the churches, and especially for Catholics, the pressing need is to consider anew what it is which they have to give to men and society; and what, as a minimal requirement, they actually need to maintain their freedom and dignity. For my part, I am extremely doubtful that religion needs the kind of public support and deference it has received in the past. Christianity has, one would assume, sufficient inner resources to survive and flourish on its own—it does not need state props, special privilege, and cultural honors. Moreover, one of the most important insights achieved by the contemporary Church is the centrality of human freedom. If it did not do so in the past, the privilege granted to religion in America (especially Christianity) now works as a limitation on the freedom of a large number of people. The extent to which the Church attempts to enlarge the freedom of those people will be the real measure of its dedication to the idea of human liberty. It costs comparatively little to argue for one's own freedom; it may cost much to argue for the freedom of another. But this latter is the meaningful test.

CHAPTER SEVEN

Secularity and Ecumenism

LIKE PEOPLE, HISTORICAL MOVEMENTS ARE SOMETIMES FORCED TO live down the gossip that their birth was illegitimate. "Secularization" and "ecumenism" have had this problem. Only recently have they gained a certain respectability in polite company. For decades, secularization was understood to mean "secularism," a God-denying, materialistic outlook which spelled doom to "spiritual values." Ecumenism was taken to mean "indifferentism," a frame of mind apt to reduce all theological differences to personal taste and to betray truth for the sake of a simpering "spirit of brotherhood."

Yet though "secularization" and "ecumenism" shared a common initial fate in the popular religious mind, their rise to respectability followed different lines. After beginning more as moods than movements, each was given a retroactive birth certificate,

57

attesting to its lineage, and each was taken up as the object of study, discussion, and enthusiasm. On the surface, the main impetus behind the ecumenical movement seemed to be the patient work of a handful of scattered theologians and journals. They argued, successfully enough, that ecumenism does not mean a compromise with truth, nor are theological and ecclesiastical convictions unimportant. Similarly, secularization engendered an attempt to show how and why it was possible for Christians to affirm the turn taken by Western history away from sacralism and an otherworldly orientation. The secularity movement (if I may so call that attempt) apparently took its rise especially from the effort of various social thinkers to convince the churches and the world that Christians could take man's terrestrial existence and welfare with full seriousness.

So far as they go, these casual explanations of the source of both movements are plausible enough. But they do not go far enough and are actually, in the broad view, somewhat misleading. Do these movements, for instance, really spring from different sources? This becomes extremely doubtful as soon as one considers the very broad cultural currents which have been stirring Western society since the end of World War II: the movement toward world unity; the growing dominance of science and technology; the evidence of a diminishing spirit of nationalism; a growing skepticism toward ideologies of any kind. Since this is the world in which most of Christianity exists, it would be positively amazing if the churches did not tend to reflect some of these same attitudes in their theologies; and of course they do. Put crudely, ecumenism is the response of the churches within their own lives to the trend toward world unity in the political sphere. Equivalently, Christian secular theology is the response of the churches to the acceptance of urban life and technology by society at large. The parallels between anti-nationalism and anti-denominationalism hardly need spelling out.

Historical explanations of this kind need not minimize the contributions made by particular thinkers and specific theological schools. But they do emphasize that theological movements have roots which are as often cultural as intellectual, as often a matter of the *zeitgeist* as of dedicated men.

That said, let me now go a step further. Not only should ecumenism and Christian secular theologies be thought of as springing from very similar origins, they are both areas of concern and speculation which we should begin treating directly as closely interrelated problems. In one way, this is already being done, at least if one heeds the common advice that, whatever their differences, Christians can and should join hands to combat the ills of racial discrimination, slums, poverty, and so on. That is good advice, but still a long way from recognizing that secularity and ecumenism are problems intimately related.

What, exactly, is the relationship? The first place worth looking for an answer is in modern history. If we can grant that Western society has in the past four hundred years or so undergone a process of secularization, then it is worth recalling the part played by the Reformation, the counter-Reformation, and the legacy of disunity. I use the word "recalling" advisedly. Men have been arguing for centuries just what, if any, responsibility Christian disunity has had for the way the modern world turned out. To avoid getting myself embroiled in these wrangles, let me simply cite the words of a diverse sampling of commentators.

Harold J. Laski, for one, has written of the Reformation, "Because it was a grave blow at authority, it loosened the hold of tradition on men's lives. Because it called into question ideas which had long held sway, it gave a deep impetus to the temper of rationalism. Both its doctrines and its social results were emancipating to the individual." [1] For Christopher Dawson, "The secularization of Western Christendom . . . involved first the loss of Christian unity, which was itself due not to secularism but to the violence of religious passion and the conflict of rival doctrines." [2]

---

[1] *The Rise of European Liberalism* (New York: Unwin Books, Barnes and Noble, 1962), p. 33.

[2] *The Historic Reality of Christian Culture* (London: Routledge and Kegan Paul, 1960), p. 19. Notice how Dawson uses the words "secularism" and "secularization" interchangeably.

As for the impact of the Reformation on political thought, the views of Karl Holl are representative of a major school of thought: "In Lutheran territories the Reformation helped that view triumph which saw in the state something superior to the individual will, an institution which served to direct all the efforts of the people. . . . At the same time it was the Reformation that first set a rigid limit to the absolute power of the state."[3] Or we may listen to Ernst Troeltsch: "The social influence of Ascetic Protestantism upon the history of civilization has been penetrating and comprehensive. Through its ecclesiastical ideal, which merges into the ideal of the Free Churches, the democratic constitution of its individual congregations, as well as of its general ecclesiastical structure, its autonomous individualism, based upon the Will of God and the fact of Redemption, and its systematic and positive industry, it has become one of the basic causes of the immense changes in modern Society."[4] And one hardly needs to mention the work of Max Weber on the economic impact of the Protestant ethos.[5]

Considerably less speculation has been lavished upon the Roman Catholic responsibility for secularization. John Courtney Murray, S.J., first became famous for his argument that Roman Catholics could accept what he called "the American proposition" because it had a long tradition which recognized the autonomy of the state, its properly secular nature and end.[6] From a different perspective, a host of Catholic writers has blamed the Church's fawning upon civil authority during the seventeenth and eighteenth centuries, for the sake of privilege and protection, as one source of an overweening pride on the part of the modern state. But examples are hard to come by here; on the whole, Roman

[3] *The Cultural Significance of the Reformation*, trans. by Karl and Barbara Hertz and John H. Lichtblau (Cleveland: World Publishing Co., Meridian Books, 1959), p. 53.

[4] *The Social Teachings of the Christian Churches*, trans. by Olive Wyon (New York: Harper Torchbook, 1960), Vol. II, p. 818.

[5] *The Protestant Ethic and the Spirit of Capitalism*, trans. by Talcott Parsons (New York: Scribners, 1930).

[6] *We Hold These Truths* (New York: Sheed & Ward, 1960).

Catholicism for some centuries set its face against the demise of the "sacral age" which had been a mark of its pre-Reformation hegemony. One might guess that its main contribution to the emergence of secularization was its tendency to praise (with necessary distinctions) what modern civilization produced, through this was usually long after the fact.[7]

There seems little doubt, however, that the continuing friction between Protestants and Catholics did much to strengthen secularization. These conflicts helped to assure the disappearance of established churches, to necessitate state neutrality toward the competing claims of the churches, to stimulate the development of secular theories of human freedom, and to allow cultural leadership to pass from religious to secular hands. I am not suggesting, in any sense, that one can explain secularization solely in these terms; at most, they were contributing causes, sometimes by commission, sometimes by omission. But taken together with industrialization, urbanization, scientific and technological progress, they played a key role. At the very least it becomes ridiculous to look upon secularization as something which came upon the churches wholly from the outside, as if it was an alien stranger for whose presence Christianity bore no responsibility.

If it is true, then, that Christian disunity has had much to do with the shaping of a secular world, it seems no less true to say that secularization has, in its turn, profoundly affected the relationship of the churches to each other. This was not true at first. As the industrial age and the nation-state came upon Western society, most forcefully in the nineteenth century, the churches were still sharply divided. Where they could, they resisted pluralism, trying with all their remaining resources to hold on to traditional prerogatives and dominance; hence in America Prot-

---

[7] See especially Jacques Maritain, *Man and the State* (Chicago: University of Chicago Press, 1951), p. 159; cf. John Courtney Murray, S.J., "The Problem of Religious Freedom," *Theological Studies*, XXV (December, 1964) One need only compare the *Syllabus of Errors* of Pope Pius IX with contemporary Roman Catholic writings to see how much of what was once condemned is now praised by Roman Catholicism.

estants resisted the coming of the Catholic immigrant, in England the established church fought a (losing) battle against the Emancipation Act, in Spain and Latin America Protestants got short shrift, and so on. Though industrialism was beginning to leave its mark, it had yet to create what Brian Wicker has aptly called "an overwhelming force towards common ideals and experience, even between the most disparate societies." [8] Though science and empiricism were coming into their own they had not yet become man's primary tool for mastering the world in which he lived. Nor had what Harvey Cox has called the "pragmatic" and "profane" style of contemporary man yet replaced the older ways of tribal and town man, much less his proclivity for metaphysical questions.[9] By and large, religion still held a lofty place. The colossus of technology cast a relatively small shadow in the beginning and only a few acute observers noticed that here and there industrialization was taking its toll among the working classes.[10]

The shadow was destined to spread. Whatever one can say about the vitality of the churches, the number of the faithful, or the creativity of theology, only a rash person would claim that institutional religion still occupies the center of the human social drama. If it is not quite proper to say that the technological mentality represents a formulated ideology, it nonetheless has created an ethos as all-encompassing as anything ever dreamed of by deliberate social planners. However much the churches might have shouted imprecations in the face of this change—from a sacral, then to a religiously pluralistic, then to a secular culture—the change came. One of the most common themes of the religious artist today is that of the small, usually gothic church surrounded by towering skyscrapers; though overdone, the image is apt enough.

[8] *Culture and Liturgy* (New York: Sheed & Ward, 1963), p. 29.
[9] See in particular *The Secular City* (New York: Macmillan, 1965), Chapter 3.
[10] For an acute analysis of how and why this happened in one English city see E. R. Wickham, *Church and People in an Industrial City* (London: Lutterworth Press, 1957), esp. Chapter 6.

What did this mean for the churches? Most notably, it meant that their own disputes, their debates over creeds and orthodoxy, their nasty disunities, became exceedingly minor struggles on the world stage. Those with a particularly religious bent of mind, or those involved in religion professionally, could lavish great passion on these matters; for the great mass of men fewer and fewer had any interest at all. Though Christians today deplore the bloody religious wars of the sixteenth century, it has at least to be said that men then took their belief as a matter of life and death. It is almost unthinkable that Christians today, whether practicing or nominal, would defend or promote their religious commitments by means of warfare. We will fight about race or borders or political methods or secular ideologies; we will not fight about religion. The optimist might credit this shift to the intrinsic good sense and charity of contemporary Christians; the realist could make a better case that ecclesiastical loyalties just don't count for that much anymore. Perhaps I should modify this last statement and just say that, though such loyalties may count, they have lost much of their old tenacity.

The net result of this shift seems clear enough. Where the churches once fought to divide the world up among themselves, they have now been forced to work for their very survival as culturally influential bodies. In the face of secularization, the struggle of one has become the struggle of all. Whether they like it or not, the Christian churches have been downgraded together to a secondary position in society. In the early days of ecumenism, one could often hear pleas that the churches patch up their quarrels for the sake of offering a common front against mutual enemies: Communism, materialism, secularism, or what have you. Nowadays one can hear a more sophisticated version of the same line of thought: that the churches have to unite to better meet the social problems of the world. Thankfully, neither the crude nor the sophisticated version has had much sway in serious ecumenical circles, but the very fact that such arguments could be put forward is adequate testimony to the displacement of Christianity as a decisive determinant of the shape of the world. One way or another, it was altogether natural for divided Christians to begin noticing that they shared an embarrassingly common lot. One observer has suggested that, faced with increased external competition, it was hardly surprising that the churches should begin banding together, that a process of religious "cartelization" should make its appearance.[11]

No less important, the impact of pluralism has been decisive for ecumenism; and pluralism is one very direct consequence of Christian disunity. In the centuries immediately following the Reformation, Europe was split roughly into two spheres. Protestantism dominated the north and Catholicism the south. To theological divisions were added geographical and cultural divisions; the likelihood of any ecumenical drive surmounting these many obstacles was slight. Only in the late nineteenth and in the twentieth century did these separations begin to diminish. The Catholic immigration to America, the coming of the Irish to Great Britain, the effect of World War II in Germany—to cite only the most prominent examples—all had the effect of placing Protestants and Catholics in physical proximity to each other. Eventually they had to find ways of living and working together, of creating a culture in which both could live in some productive way, and of theologically justifying the new relationship forced upon them.

At first it was exceedingly difficult to do these things, but with time, experience, and a gradual acceptance of the reality of pluralism the sharper edges of conflict were honed away. There still exist many Protestant-Catholic conflicts over issues of Church and State, but they are now remarkably mild when compared with past decades. The reduction of earlier political tensions has, in its turn, created a favorable environment for a reduction of theological differences. Indeed, since Protestants and Catholics increasingly share a common cultural, social, and political life in most Western nations, their only significant divisions are coming to be theological. One might say that the upheaval of the sixteenth century has now come full circle: what began as a theological dispute and then

[11] I am indebted to Professor Peter Berger of the New School for this intriguing idea.

degenerated into a religio-political cold (and sometimes hot) war has once again become theological. The great success of recent Protestant-Catholic dialogue would indicate that theological oppositions are far easier to overcome than cultural and political divisions; that should be a valuable lesson for the future as well as a major vindication of the value of pluralism for Christian life.[12]

Yet to point to some of the valuable off-shoots of secularization for the progress of ecumenism by no means exhausts the complexity of their relationship. If nothing else, these off-shoots have usually been accidental, often resisted by the churches and rarely appropriated in a creative way at the outset. It is easy enough to concede after the fact that secularization has not been the disaster the churches imagined it might be. It will be far more difficult to take the next steps: to anticipate the changes which secularization will undoubtedly continue to bring, to shape a viable, flexible and continuing Christian response, and—hopefully— to make some difference to the possible directions which secularization can take.

That many such attempts are now being made should be apparent to anyone even vaguely familiar with recent Christian thought. Not all of these attempts are favorable to the emergence of secularization. The work of Christopher Dawson and T. S. Eliot [13] provides an example of two sensitive men intent on showing the necessity of re creating some form (however updated) of Christian civilization. The ideology of the conservative thinkers grouped around the *National Review* and *Modern Age* is heavily prone to emphasize the enduring validity of the idea of "the Christian West." On a more popular level, the outcries directed against recent Supreme Court decisions on prayer and Bible-reading lay major stress on the evils of a "Godless" and "secularistic" society. And as one articulate writer put it, "The harmony . . . between religion, military courage and science, is responsible for

[12] Cf. H. Richard Niebuhr, *The Social Sources of Denominationalism* (Cleveland: World Publishing Co., Meridian Books, 1957), p. 270.

[13] Dawson, *The Historic Reality of Christian Culture*; and T. S. Eliot, *The Idea of a Christian Society* (London: Faber and Faber, 1939).

the noble character which all nations have hailed with universal acclamation. . . . Take the first element away from it, and the unity, or in other words, the whole beauty of it, disappears." These last words were not written, as one might reasonably guess, by a God-fearing patriot urging the United States to stem the tide of atheistic Communism, but by a spiritual ancestor of that breed, Joseph DeMaistre.[14] A contemporary of DeMaistre expressed the ultimate fear: "The day when the atheistic dogma of the sovereignty of the people replaces in politics the sacred dogma of the sovereignty of God; the day when Europe ceases to be Christian and monarchical, she will perish, and the sceptre of the world will pass to other hands." [15] As it happened, Europe did not perish, but "the sceptre of the world" did "pass to other hands"—to the increasingly worldwide dominion of technology and (incipiently at least) to the newly emergent Afro-Asian lands, however odd this juxtaposition may seem. A constant premise of contemporary conservative thought is that a spiritual disease is at hand if this movement is not reversed—by spiritual means, if possible; by force, if necessary.

The positive response to secularization has been equally varied, though it too shares some common premises. They are, roughly: a) that technology and material progress are to be welcomed and fostered; b) that the demise of monarchical Europe and its attendant assumption of a well-merited Christian spiritual hegemony has proved to be a source of human liberation; c) that political, psychological, cultural, and religious freedom are necessary conditions for human development; and d) that Christianity will be faithful to its essential nature only insofar as it affirms the dignity of the material world and contributes to humanity's temporal well-being. Other premises might well be detected, but I think there would be some general agreement on those suggested.

[14] "War, Peace, and Social Order" (1852), in *Catholic Political Thought 1789–1848*, edited by Bela Menczer (Notre Dame, Ind.: University of Notre Dame Press, 1962), p. 62.
[15] Vicomte De Bonald, "The Unity of Europe" (1799), in Menczer, *op. cit.*, pp. 88–89.

All would not be rejected by conservative thinkers, but some probably would; and those accepted might be seen in a very different
light than is common to Christian secular thought.

As could be expected, the strategies which have been devised
from these premises vary to a considerable degree. Some, like Harvey Cox in *The Secular City*, are apt to seek a rich Christian
appropriation of just those aspects of contemporary secularization
most despised: mobility, anonymity, pragmatism, organization-life,
a love of the profane. Others are more prone to stress the alienation, rootlessness, and demonic side of present-day life, pressing
all the while toward the vision of a new society which transcends
both the *ancien régime* (in its rigid and modified forms) and the
crushing embrace of a technocratic world. Still others, like Teil-
hard de Chardin and many of his followers, seem to believe that
in the very nature of things man and matter are moving inexorably toward the Omega point; it is less a matter of strategy than of
acceptance and perception. Some, like Karl Rahner, welcome the
advent of secularization but emphasize less the creation of a new
man and a new society than the necessity for the Christians'
acceptance of their "diaspora situation" and the establishment of
a qualitative rather than quantitative witness to salvific truths.[16]
And then there are a few who believe, with Paul Van Buren, that
the main job at hand is to find "the secular meaning of the
Gospel."

Whatever the different strategies, however, and whatever the
common premises, our attention is being called to certain facts.
One of these facts—though it is boring by now to use the word—
is the lack of Christian "relevance" to the complex, urbane, con-
fusing human situation of the second half of the twentieth century. Another is that man seems to be making a decent go of a
life where religion may still capture his nominal allegiance but
does not grip and animate his imagination. Another is that where
religion is not irrelevant it too often falls into an equally bad pit,
that of providing transcendent sanction and legitimation for the

[16] *The Christian Commitment*, trans. by Cecily Hastings (New York:
Sheed & Ward, 1963), esp. Chapter 1.

political status quo. Another is that technology and urbanization are here to stay and that religion had better make the most of it. Finally—and here I will add my own assertion of what is a "fact" —that nothing could matter much less to contemporary man than the truth about justification, papal infallibility, *agape*, Mary's heavenly titles, the relationship of Scripture and tradition; in short, just about everything that the most serious and dedicated ecumenical scholars would find worthy of a life's work.

This last fact, if it can be accepted as such, points to a sobering conclusion. Even if the most exalted dream of total Christian reunion could be achieved, there is no longer any certainty that it would have a decisive influence on the future of the world. Despite all the progress which ecumenism has made, it would be difficult to argue that this has significantly changed the relationship of nations, affected the quality of most human encounters, altered the character of urban or rural life, or has solved in any way whatsoever the problems posed by automation, cybernation, nuclear power, and the imbalance of rich and poor nations. If my earlier assumption is correct—that ecumenism is as much the result of social change as of theological illumination—then one could almost say that what happens in the world will make far more difference to the churches than the converse.

One might reply to this that ecumenism is still so new and tentative that to expect any immediate decisive influence on the world would be precipitous; it is enough to hope and work for this influence and leave the rest in the hands of God. This is a good retort, for that matter very disarming. But one would at least like to see some preliminary hints that this hope has some foundation in reality. If there are such hints they are surely "preliminary" in the extreme: the effectiveness of an ecumenical witness in the area of American race relations (an effectiveness, however, which has presupposed and built upon a prior legal and political consensus whose origin is heavily secular); the effectiveness of an ecumenical witness against the horrors of nuclear warfare (but an effectiveness, again, whose roots are the very human fears and anxieties about physical destruction); the symbolic value for mankind as a whole of two antagonistic forces beginning to patch up their differences after four hundred years of tension and suspicion (but a symbol whose value is diminished when one realizes that historical and sociological changes have been as important as charity and understanding).

Nonetheless, however much one may be able to qualify the various contributions of ecumenism to the general problems which torment, divide, and hinder the human race, they may be the only kind which ecumenism can offer. More specifically, ecumenism can provide mankind with little in the way of direct help, but may be able to make many indirect contributions, the sum total of which could be significant. There are three ways (minimally) this could be done: 1. by stimulating the inner renewal of the churches, thus fortifying and enriching their perception, appropriation, and witness of Christ; 2. by making possible the formation of broad Christian pressure groups whose strength can be brought to bear, together with other groups, in the formation of political and social policy; 3. by providing the world with a model of the ways in which men whose divisions are deep can go about achieving reconciliation.

The value of each of these contributions can be spelled out very briefly. It is a principle common to all Christians that Christ came to redeem the world, but that this redemption must be carried on and extended by the Church; hence the need for inner renewal if this work is to be done. There is now a general agreement that in highly organized yet socially fragmented societies political and social developments require the kinds of pressure which strong individual groups, or coalition groups can bring to bear on the body politic; hence, the need for Christian "pressure groups" (in the non-pejorative sense) working in alliance with others. Finally, it should be clear that mankind has made only small progress in the direction of developing techniques for the reduction of nationalistic antagonisms, ideological confrontations, racial, ethnic, and class hostilities; hence, the great need for some useful models or examples of communities which have devised methods of overcoming long-standing hostilities. Expressed in the most primitive terms possible, ecumenism would have much to give the world if mankind could point to divided Christians and say: see how they love each other despite their differences; see how they can work together for the good of mankind; see how they each strive to live up to the highest ideals of their respective traditions; see how they are able, in peace, to work through their disputes.

To the extent that the process of secularization continues, to that extent will the world require the particular gifts which an ecumenical Christianity can offer. While there are many indications of a trend toward world unity, they are indications only. Practically speaking, the spirit of nationalism has been one consequence of secularization; national groupings have come in great measure to replace religious groupings. The realization of world unity will necessitate that the nations learn to get along with each and to find the means whereby their narrower allegiances can be transmuted into broader, more universal bonds. Again, secularization has done its part in the movement toward urbanization. Yet for all its worth, urbanization poses serious dangers to personal identity, to a sense of human community, and to the possibility of man dominating his environment. Still again, secularization has often meant a diminishment of man's search for some abiding realities, for some ultimate meaning behind human life. By enlarging and deepening the contributions which an ecumenical Christianity can make to man's quest for his own significance, it is possible to hope that the dangers of secularization can be lessened.

More importantly, it is possible to hope that an ecumenical Christianity can help mankind to realize the inherent strengths and possibilities of secularization. To my mind, one of the most useful sketches of the characteristics of secularization has been presented by D. L. Munby in *The Idea of a Secular Society*.[17] Let me simply quote Munby on "the marks of a secular society" and add some suggestions of my own about appropriate ecumenical responses.

[17] (London: Oxford University Press, 1963).

"(a) A secular society is one which explicitly refuses to commit itself as a whole to any particular view of the nature of the universe and the place of man in it." [18] This should pose no special problems for Christians. They, above all, should know from their own history how much mischief was done by the attempts of the churches to impose their pattern of belief and practice at the expense of religious liberty. At the same time, ecumenical Christianity should point out to mankind that truth matters and that the individual has the human duty to try and discover what the universe means and who he, as man, is. It should also resist, as part of its prophetic task, the attempt by any church, ideology, or faction to impose its own world-view on everyone.

"(b) Such a society is unlikely to be homogeneous, and we do not find homogeneity." [19] Ecumenical Christians should welcome this lack of homogeneity. It will be a reflection, at one level, of the diversity of human gifts, temperaments, personal experience, and different assimilations of the truth. At another level, it will reflect the actual freedom open to persons to seek, express, and witness their own reading of the universe and what it requires of them. Given a natural human diversity, the presence of homogeneity in a society may be taken as *prima facie* evidence that freedom is lacking. It would, however, be very curious for ecumenical Christians to assert in some dogmatic fashion that no common values should be sought or desired; they would thereby be denying that their own beliefs have anything more than local, subjective, and idiosyncratic value.

"(c) A secular society is a tolerant society. It makes no attempt to enforce beliefs or to limit the expression of belief. . . . [It] expressly tries to draw boundaries between public and private morality, and to widen the sphere of private decision and private choice." [20] My comments on (a) and (b) are pertinent here as well, but an additional point is also in order. If ecumenical Christians are serious about the centrality of religious liberty,

[18] *Ibid.*, p. 14.
[19] *Ibid.*, p. 17.
[20] *Ibid.*, p. 20.

both for the good of individuals and the integrity of the churches, then they have equally to realize that such liberty demands the presence of as many serious options as possible. Spain and the Soviet Union have a theoretical religious liberty; but the practical choices available to individuals make this liberty null and void. Protestants and Catholics should not work only for the freedom of choosing between Protestantism and Catholicism but also for the freedom of choosing between secular humanism and Christianity, atheism and belief, and so forth.

"(d) Any society must have some common aims, in the sense that people are doing things together to produce certain effects. . . . In order to produce these effects there must be organization, an agreed method of solving problems, and a common framework of law. There must be political institutions, a legal system, and an economic organization. . . . in a secular society these organizations and institutions have limited aims—at least in principle" [21] Among other things, Mr. Munby is here saying that politicians, legislators, and judges should not be allowed to function as the "architects of manners and morals" or as "prophet-priests of the national conscience." [22] This is an astute observation and one which should be appreciated by ecumenical Christians aware of the way in which sacral Christianity (whether of the medieval or post-Reformation variety) endowed law-givers and magistrates with the power to coerce consciences and to shape society in ways determined by the churches. People will be free insofar as political leaders do not attempt to impose an over-arching value system. Whether this is done in the name of Christian values or anti-Christian values is irrelevant; in either case human dignity will be lessened. Still, it must be said that some degree of unity and shared values is necessary for a stable and viable society. The Christian contribution should be that of keeping before the eye of the public basic human needs: the needs for liberty, peace, food, job, family stability, social justice, adequate clothes, and housing. Ecumenical Christianity can also serve the unity of society by exer-

[21] *Ibid.*, p. 23.
[22] *Ibid.*, p. 25.

cising its power of reconciliation, its ability to cut across class lines, and its potentiality to perceive where men differ and where they agree.

"(e) In such a world we have discovered how various are the problems that can be solved by examination of the facts." [23] If nothing else, the ecumenical movement has demonstrated the value of hard, impartial investigation of Christian disunity; one need mention only the profound effect of recent Roman Catholic studies of the Reformation. Beyond this parochial matter, empirical examination has established its validity in every domain. Christianity has a special stake in promoting its wider use: it helps to destroy harmful myths about man, religion, and society and it helps to locate the genuine problems.[24] Yet it would not be impertinent for ecumenical Christianity to remind those overly enamored with data and statistics that man has secret recesses in his heart which cannot be charted on graphs; that despite all the predictions which can be made about his behavior, man remains a mystery.

"(f) A secular society is a society without official images. If there are no common aims, there cannot be a common set of images reflecting the common ideals and emotions of everyone. Nor can there be any common ideal types of behavior for universal application." [25] This particular mark of a secular society presents some difficulties. To say that a secular society requires that

---

[23] *Ibid.*, p. 25.

[24] " 'Don't think, but look!' was Wittgenstein's repeated advice to his students. It should be taken to heart by all expositors of religion. As applied to Christianity in particular, no amount of laborious excogitation can answer the basic question: What is the evidence? And what is its value?" Dom Aelred Graham, "The Pathos of Vatican II," *Encounter* XXV (December, 1965), p. 19.

[25] Munby, *op. cit.*, pp. 30–31. It is worth noting a comment made by Anson Phelps Stokes on the origin of the expression "In God We Trust": ". . . this familiar motto on our coins was the direct result of the crisis through which the country was passing during the Civil War, and was an evidence of the feeling that the nation needed to cultivate the spirit of religion." *Church and State in the United States,* revised edition, by Anson Phelps Stokes and Leo Pfeffer (New York: Harper & Row, 1964), pp. 568–569.

there be no official images makes considerable practical sense; images can dominate men almost as effectively as dogmas and rituals. But it seems to me something else again to accept passively the absence of any common aims. If human beings do have the needs I suggested above, and some right to expect society to help them to satisfy these needs, then there must be a minimal set of common aims. A society where people did not seek justice for all and did not maintain the ideal of justice would be an unhealthy society; it could be positively barbarian. So, too, for a society in which people did not hold to the ideal of human beings taking concern for each other's welfare. Beyond considerations of that kind, it is almost inconceivable that a society could for long exist in which those who made it up shared no ideals at all. How could one, for instance, hope to maintain a legal system in the absence of a shared evaluation that a certain degree of lawfulness is essential for the sake of civic peace? The question, really, is how far Christians should press for some common civic and social ideals, and what kind they should press for, and how far they should promote the establishment of private visions of the good life and the good society. Out of respect for the common ideal of decent brevity, I will not try to answer that question here.

Mr. Munby concludes his description by saying, "The positive ideals that lie behind the idea of the secular society are firstly a deep respect for the individual man and the small groups of which society is made up." [26] This seems to me as good a thumbnail sketch as any. Just how closely this ideal tallies with a major impetus of the ecumenical movement should, I trust, require no special elucidation.

What will the future bring? Historically, the roots of secularization appear to be deeper and more extensive than those of ecumenism. It is conceivable, though highly unlikely, that ecumenism could lose its present drive and become once again only the concern of a few specialists. But it is almost inconceivable that the movement toward secularization could reverse itself; and that because it is so much a result of urban and technological changes

[26] Munby, *op. cit.*, p. 33

which now seem permanent. In any case, at the moment ecumenism and secularization are solidly entrenched. Sociologically and culturally, the latter provides the human context for the former. Just as the turns taken by society in the past were crucial for Christian relations, so they are likely to remain in the future. The main difference now, however, is that Christians are in a position to profit from, rather than instinctively resist, these turns. This can only be done in the present situation by recognizing the mutual impact which ecumenism and secularization can have on each other. To think that ecumenism can be carried on independent of contemporary culture would be naive. To think that ecumenism has no special duties toward broader human concerns would be irresponsible.

CHAPTER EIGHT

The Secular City

ORDINARILY, THERE IS NOTHING SO HARD FOR THE RELIGIOUS MAN to cope with as social change. It sets him to twitching, worrying, and desperately attempting to squeeze from Scripture some measure of solace. Now and then he may try to find a way of turning the change to his advantage, or see some faintly redeeming possibilities in cultural earthquakes. But his more common response is denunciation of the new. He feels threatened, and his instant reaction is defensive and abusive. Historically, he has some reason to feel this way. Massive social change inevitably affects the religious life of a society. The shift from feudalism to capitalism in the West is as good an instance as any of what can happen. Entrepreneurs, not bishops, began to call the tune. Troubled believers felt they could only hum a dirge.

Of late there has been a shift in this pattern. During the past couple of decades one theologian after another has come forward to reluctantly bless scientific, technological and economic advances. They have learned at least one lesson from their predecessors' mistakes: no amount of ecclesiastical railing can do much to stop social upheavals. The way to survive is to hang on for dear life, all the while looking for some way of legitimately baptizing the new tiger. The theologian may not always like what he has to do, but at least he does it. He smiles bravely and gets to work.

Harvey Cox is very much a part of this new mode, only he goes one step further, ecstatically hailing contemporary social change as the occasion for a revitalized Christianity. As much as anything, it is probably this fetching enthusiasm which accounts for the reception being given his book *The Secular City* (Macmillan, 1965). Eagerly passed from hand to hand, quickly adopted by a variety of study groups, it has all the earmarks of a religious *cause célèbre*. It must, then, be meeting some deep need: the longing for a persuasive and unembarrassed theology of secularity. Many attempts have been made in this direction, but almost all of them suffer from the debilitating drawback of treating secularity as a religious disaster—a redeemable disaster, but still a disaster. There is no hint of this in Cox's book.

The key to its power lies in his almost rapturous love for two characteristic features of our age: secularization and urbanization. This won't commend the book to some, but Cox starts from a premise hard to dismiss, *what is*. Far from running their course, secularity and the city are just beginning to take hold. There are always strategies available to evade the impact of historical trends: one can work for the return of a golden age, or fashion utopias, or just withdraw into private metaphysical enclosures, seeking an other-worldly transcendence. Cox will have none of this. His method is to look squarely in the eye that face of contemporary life which most offends the religious and cultural savants; and then to say: you are good, and if you are not we can make you so.

The much bemoaned anonymity of urban life, for instance, Cox hails. It provides the possibility of an historically unparalleled freedom from social convention and culturally enforced mores. Mobility and rootlessness provide like possibilities: a liberation from the smothering embrace of small-town provincialism. Another omnipresent bogeyman of the wise, the modern organization, is no less extolled. Better that structure of human relationships and purposes, with its flexibility, secularized goals, orientation toward the future and limited claims upon its members than a sacred order with its enslavement to the past and its deification of law and custom.

Cox's treatment of "secularization" is unflinching. Defining it as "the liberation of man from religious and metaphysical tutelage, the turning of his attention away from other worlds and toward this one," he defends its human values and claims that its roots are biblical. How is this possible? Cox's argument rests on three points. There is the disenchantment of nature stemming from the Hebraic conception of creation; the desacralization of politics arising from a separation of the political and religious order; and the deconsecration of values which issues from the Jewish relativizing of human values and their representations. Thus was the way opened for a "constructive relativism," which "allows secular man to note the transience and relativity of all cultural creations and of every value system without sinking into the abyss of nihilism." From these roots the technological-urban tree was able to spring.

The cumulative result is a secular man who is pragmatic and profane: "Life for him is a set of problems, not an unfathomable mystery. He brackets off the things that cannot be dealt with and deals with those that can. He wastes little time thinking about 'ultimate' or 'religious' questions. And he can live with highly provisional solutions." Just the kind of man, in other words, who is the despair of Sunday preachers. Not so for Cox, whose book shows the decisive impact of Bonhoeffer. "The Gospel," he writes, "does not call men to return to a previous stage of his development. It does not summon man back to dependence, awe and religiousness. Rather it is a call to imaginative urbanity and creative secularity." Just as the city has replaced the town, so also should the political replace the metaphysical as the context of human thought.

Are there any clouds on the horizon? Very many, but none which are incapable of human mastery given intelligence, planning, and the full freedom of the Gospel. The role of the Church is not to change the present historical direction of society, but to exercise its power of cultural exorcism, its mission of reconciliation, its potentialities as an avant-garde for the Kingdom of God.

"God"? One might well inquire at this point just how God fits into this secularized world. Having dismissed metaphysics, Cox is not tempted to create a new natural theology. Instead he asserts that the word "God" has no meaning for secular man; and he implies that even the Christian is not very certain what it means. But shouldn't this at least be a source of discomfort, or even of those existential paroxysms which Cox deplores? Not at all, for God has often hidden Himself for a time, choosing to reveal His name only gradually "through the abrasive experiences of social change. . . . Perhaps, like Moses, we must simply take up the work of liberating the captives, confident that we will be granted a new name by the events of the future."

All of this is a rich pudding, especially from a Protestant minister and professor who in an earlier age would have been called a "divine." But it adds up to a coherent whole, however questionable many of the pieces. By and large, it makes considerably more sense than some of the speculation to be found in a recent volume of the *Concilium* series, *The Church and the World*, edited by Johannes B. Metz (Paulist Press, 1965). This is painful to say, because the purpose of the volume is to chart the new frontiers of Catholic thought. The problem is not that the *Concilium* volume lacks boldness or even originality, but that many of the authors are still too much caught up in metaphysical, existentialist, or personalist quandaries.

A reading of Cox's book has *almost* convinced me that the day of such problems has passed. However pertinent for some aspects of human existence, a relentless concentration on them contributes very little to the creation of viable social structures and mastery of the material world. It is to continue, in other terms, the traditional quest for the absolute—whether that be construed as a grasp of the totality of being, the nature of existence, or the essence of persons. All too easily this plays into the hands of those who can't stand the problematical, the functional, the pragmatic, the experimental. They are essentially "religious" searches, at least if religion is understood as a hunt for the permanent in the face of the transitory, of ultimate meaning amidst uncertainty. Too often they are concerns which tend to keep alive some old and dangerous dualities, even if that is not their intention.

The persistence of dualism can be seen in a distinction Monsignor Gerard Philips commends in his essay in *The Church and the World*. "Catholics," he says, "are learning to make a clearer distinction between their strictly ecclesial mission and the mature program of action they have to realize now in the world." Heaven help us if they are. What Monsignor Philips does not seem to notice is that a sharp sundering of the spiritual and the temporal leads to an egregious type of Christian utilitarianism: man should be served, not for his own sake, but for that of the Church. As he revealingly puts it, the Church "could not perform its primary mission if it did not rouse in its members, in behalf of all their human brethren, a spirit of disinterested mutual help." This kind of thinking has been the source of the Church's failure to demonstrate that it is fully able to help build a humane social order. It is nothing less than a gentle way of saying that the Church's ultimate interests lie elsewhere, thus forgetting that when man is slighted for the sake of God, God will soon be slighted also.

Equally mistaken, though less hazardous, is Hans Urs von Balthasar's assertion in the same volume that a "demythologized" and "dephilosophized" theology "would have nothing more to do with the totality of being." "Of necessity," he says, "it could only present itself as a solace for the anguished existential subject." I must confess I can't discover where this "necessity" lies. The whole point of trying to rid theology of dead myths and an excessive dependence upon philosophical modes of thought is to better grasp the essence of the biblical message in its own terms, and from there to learn something about man's condition. One major fruit of this effort has been the discovery that the Bible is far more than the husk of hidden eternal truths. It is a record of man's encounter with God: a God who reveals Himself in history rather than in the philosopher's study, a God who speaks through the language of events rather than that of timeless essences.

Put abstractly like this, there are probably few Catholic theologians who would sharply dissent. I am merely saying what it has now become fashionable to say. Yet if one looks to find evidence of a new creativity in dealing with man's historical and political life, one is most likely to discover only a new set of abstractions. One might expect, for instance, to find the Catholic sociologist or psychologist accorded a stature equal to that of the theologian. Or to find that the natural and social sciences, which deal with matter and man in their empirical grittiness, dominating the advance guard of Catholic thought. This is not the case at all. Most of the great Catholic figures of our day—the Rahners, the Küngs, the Schillebeeckxs, the von Balthasars—are notably scant in references to economics, political science, urban planning, and even to the sociology and psychology of religion.

What they have done, and what the Church has honored them for, is to substitute new theologies for old theologies. That is a worthwhile project for those concerned with the intricacies of the Christian revelation; and some people should be. But it is also a graphic illustration of why even the freshest Catholic theology has the same mark of irrelevance as did its forerunners. It is essentially turned in upon itself, and nowhere more obviously than when it tries to talk about "the world" exclusively in the language of theology. The new realm of Catholic thought—of I-thou encounters, salvation history, omega points, Lonergan-like insight, *sein* and *dasein*, kerygma—is a delightful place for Catholics to live. It's just that we're the only ones who live there, along with a few scattered Protestants. The rest of the world lives somewhere else and our new jargon is just as esoteric and beside the point outside the family circle as the old.

I say this out of a vast sense of frustration. Give or take a few setbacks, the recent progress of Catholic theological thought has been nothing less than spectacular. But I see little evidence that it will come to mean anything more to secular man than did the old scholastic panoply of clear and certain ideas. I am secular man, too, and my Catholic brothers are legion.

In an otherwise excellent article in *America* on Christian secularity, Father Thomas E. Clarke, S.J., felt compelled to caution that "the distinction between *sacred* and *secular* is beyond question." There we have the central issue: is this distinction actually beyond doubt? If it is, then it is almost certainly hopeless to expect that secular man will ever know what the Christian is talking about. Equally hopeless would be an expectation that the Christian secular man could come to know how to construct a coherent human life. As long as he feels that life for him necessarily entails walking some delicate tight-rope between the sacred and secular, the natural and the supernatural, the redeemed and the unredeemed, he will always be dizzy. He won't and can't go off into the desert; but then he will always worry whether he can be as totally committed to man's life on earth as the most ardent atheist.

I don't think this is a fictitious or outdated problem. Some of the most disturbed Catholics I have run across recently are those who have heeded the Church's call to serve the world and then have found, once they started doing so, that their Christianity ceased to have much meaning for them. They discovered that the work of the world seems to carry its own intrinsic justification, requiring neither religious motives nor religious goals. A shock of this kind is only natural to those exhorted for years to maintain a balance between sacred and secular—and all the more so when they have been told that the secular world has no final meaning.

Far more illuminating is a perspective on God and man which sees man's temporal concerns and drives as one with his spiritual destiny. The central meaning of the Incarnation, I take it, is that Christ *has* redeemed man and matter. If this is so, then the sacred and the secular have entered into a relationship of unity; not a perfect or complete unity, but surely enough to render any talk of their radical difference highly misleading. Worse than that, a desire to maintain the distinction forces one to follow Monsignor

Philips' route into the wilderness of primary and secondary ecclesial missions, of separating love of God from love of man. Once into that jungle there is no way out.

Yet Cox's stance has some equally imposing difficulties to overcome. Can secular man, after all, afford to ignore metaphysics? Can he really get away with a purely pragmatic solution to his socio-historical problems? Up to a point, I think the answer is yes to both questions. It has to be yes, because many men patently manage to live anti-metaphysical, pragmatic lives and seem to be none the worse for it. The Christian may look at such a man with skepticism and incredulity, but there are many secular men who can confound his pessimistic expectations.

The question, then, is not whether such men can exist, and exist happily—they just do—but whether mankind as a whole can live this way either now or in the future? Let me say that I personally don't know; it would be silly to say anything else. At the same time, it also has to be said that decisions have consequences. The pragmatic decisions taken by this generation for the sake of its own life will inevitably affect, if not decisively shape, the life of future generations. The past has always imposed its relativities upon the future, and it is likely to continue doing so. The pragmatic man who does not recognize this will be a dangerous man. But as soon as he does see that his decisions will have consequences, and tries responsibly to take this fact into account, he will cease to be wholly pragmatic. He will have no other choice. One way or the other, he will have to dip his toe into the murky waters of metaphysics. He will have to fashion at least some tentative conclusions about what is good for man regardless of his specific historical situation. He will have to say what minimal conditions are necessary for human freedom, existence, and fulfillment.

Cox would have the Christian "unreservedly contextual" in his ethics and in his evangelism. Yet if the responsible secular man can't be all that contextual himself, it is difficult to see how the Christian can either. What Cox wants is a Christian who knows how to respond to his present age; how to unencumber himself of an anachronistic past; how to speak to the here and now; how to lay the ground for the future. These are fine goals, but each of them actually requires the ability to get out of one's context, at least some of the time. Cox himself does this when he speaks warmly of a "biblical perspective" on the world; or when he uses the imagery of the "kingdom of God." These are categories which cut across time and through history. They illuminate the contextual without themselves being wholly contextual.

Ironically, of course, once Cox begins using biblical language, he cuts himself off from secular man. Here, I think, Cox has to fish or cut bait. If secular man and his way of life are self-sufficient, any talk about taking a "biblical perspective" is beside the point. Who needs it, and so what, anyway? The only possible reason for bothering would be that even at its utopian best the world of secular man will have its nether regions. The *Playboy* bachelor can make the most of urban anonymity; not everyone else can. Mobility is grand if one has brains and a future; not everyone does. And so on. The urban-secular coin has two sides—and so does man.

Had Cox recognized this more clearly, he might well have been less cavalier toward those caught up in existential anguish. One reason for their plight is the often oppressive weight of the present. There are times when life is just awful: boring, stupid, brutal, or trivial. The promise of the future does not always, nor can it, drive out the pain of the present. Some people are going to die tomorrow. That is their context, and they want to know why. This is a very personal question, not something that history of sociology or politics can throw much light on. A question like this is wretchedly ultimate, direct, and non-contextual. It just won't go away.

An obvious conclusion at this point would be to say that the upshot is something of a draw. Those who would have men put aside metaphysics, existentialism, and the higher speculations of personalism in favor of politics, sociology, and history have the temper of modern man on their side. They are also in a better position to turn directly to immediate human needs, unencumbered by any pressing demand to work out final values and goals. On the other hand, man is not just a political and historical creature; he does not live by social reconstruction alone. Someone has to speak to the non-historical self, and never more so than when all of a man's plans and hopes come to nothing or when he looks death in the face. Thus can the ball be volleyed back and forth.

Still, I suspect that a choice has to be made. Ideally, it should be possible for humans to turn their attention simultaneously toward metaphysics and social planning. Psychologically, this is difficult to manage. Historically, the Christian's obsession with ultimacy has meant a debasement of the temporal. Even when he tried to take his present moment seriously, his theological concerns would not allow him to do so. His orientation toward an eternal future kept him in bondage to the historical past; the world was always outrunning him. Once again it is outrunning him. His only hope of catching up, I'm afraid, is to let go. To let go of his desire for immediate meaning. To let go of his wish for religious security. To let go of his need to see the hand of God. To let go of the quest for a new vision, or the revivification of the old one.

I suppose this is almost too much to ask of the Christian. But if the Christian cannot wait for God, if the Christian cannot make the course of history his own, if the Christian cannot give himself unreservedly to man and his temporal existence—then it is hard to see how he will ever live in the present, much less speak to it. There are many ways of gaining the whole world while losing one's soul. There are also many ways of gaining one's soul and losing the world. The world we stand to lose is the world Christ redeemed.

PART III

Forming the Laity

CHAPTER NINE

Freedom and the Layman

IF IT IS TRUE, AS KARL RAHNER HAS WRITTEN, THAT "THE LAYMAN is a Christian who remains in the world," it might then follow that a layman would be wise to discuss freedom from his vantage point in that world. More than common prudence commends this course. For it is daily borne in upon a layman that he is caught between two realms. On the one hand, there is the accumulated wisdom of the Church, conveyed to him in his religious education, through the liturgy, in sermons, and in exhortations. To this may be added the growing body of literature on the "theology of the layman." On the other, there is the accumulated wisdom of the secular world; here is another master which daily instructs him. Ideally, the Church should give the layman some insight into the meaning of that world in which he lives. This the Church does. Practically speaking, however, it often happens that the world in turn gives the layman some insight into the meaning of the

Church. There is really nothing odd in this, much less anything improper. The wise man will take his wisdom wherever he finds it; and so should the Church.

It is at once possible to see that the contemporary pertinence of the subject "Freedom and the Layman" tells us as much about the world as it does about the Church. History is not just a series of accidents, whether it is a matter of secular or ecclesiastical history. And here history shows us that the emerging consciousness of twentieth-century man has come to center on the idea of freedom. The sources of this emergence are many. There is, in impulse at least, a movement away from paternalistic societies, stimulated in great part by the spread of education, rising economic expectations, and democratic ideals throughout the world. Even the most autocratic political regimes feel compelled to pay homage to the goal of the self-directing free man in a free society. This movement toward human autonomy has been powerfully prodded by the disastrous consequences of man's recent experience with totalitarian governments. There is, quite rightly, a deep and pervasive suspicion of any theory of government which assumes that men should place their fate totally in the hands of others. This does not mean that men do not in fact still do so; but as general theories paternalistic ideologies have come on hard days.

Closely related to this development is an awakening consciousness of the responsibility of the person to make his own moral decisions. In the Nuremberg trials and in the case of Adolf Eichmann, the world saw the utterly evil consequences of an ethic which enables men to excuse their crimes against humanity on the grounds that they are only "following orders." Here were men— men as self-excusing animals—who claimed that they had no obligation to determine matters of right and wrong. Their only duty, as they saw it, was to be loyal and obedient servants of the regime to which they had pledged allegiance. The moral, for those who would call themselves free men, was clear: there is no cause, no loyalty, no set of principles which can justify any person who would claim he is not responsible for his actions. None of us can hand over our moral decisions to another.

Still another source of the emergence of freedom as the rallying cry of our day is the suffocating presence of mass societies. We no longer live in a world of scattered individuals clustered together in small groups surrounded by unmapped wilderness and virgin forests. Now there are people everywhere, so many indeed that it is more and more difficult for the individual to keep himself from being swallowed up in an endless sea of nameless humanity. Impersonal economic, political, sociological forces frighten and coerce us. Faced with such forces, personal initiative, personal identification, and personal freedom are sought with desperate energy. So too, in such a world, there is much talk of self-fulfillment, honesty, integrity, authenticity—talk, that is, of anything which will help the isolated person retain some vital sense of his uniqueness, his right to existence, his worth and destiny.

There is a connecting thread which binds together the seemingly disparate movements and events which are shaking the contemporary world. The African who rebels against colonialism is moved by many of the same deep forces which impel the Negro in Harlem to force out white merchants. The novelist who glorifies a life of sexual abandon and despises the mores of middle-class monogamy shares a certain kinship with the Christian social reformer who would uproot a system of exploitation based on ritualistically accepted economic values. Each protests against a passive acquiescence to unexamined cultural values. The local Communist party leader who desires some degree of independence from Moscow is stirred by a spirit not wholly unlike that which leads many students today to rebel against authority. The connecting thread in all of these instances is a surge toward freedom, however misguided and naive may be the forms it takes.

Freedom is in the bones of modern man; one way or another it will find expression. He wants freedom from hunger, from political domination, from the impersonal weight of oppressive custom and ritualistically sustained values. He wants freedom to plan his own life, to make his own decisions, to find that mode and direction of life which will enable him to realize his full human dignity. But modern man is also skeptical, less given to utopian dreams, less prone to place his faith in charismatic leaders, less willing to commit himself blindly to the panaceas of those who would call themselves wise. He is often a rebel, burned and scarred by the ravages of too many holy wars, too many causes turned sour, too many dreams shattered. To be sure, in moments of fear or in moments of sudden vision, the rebel in him may give way to the conformist or the enthusiast; but the rebel is still there, ready to reappear when calm returns or the vision fades. Above all, he wants to be himself, and that self he has found can only be achieved through freedom.

What, in the judgment of modern man, are the conditions necessary to insure this freedom he seeks? One can discern something approaching a consensus in answer to this question. At its focal point is the possibility of making choices. The measure of freedom is the psychological capacity to choose between alternative possibilities, and the presence of genuine options from which to choose. There is a desire for political freedom—the freedom to choose among a variety of political goals, programs and leaders. There is a desire for social freedom—the freedom to choose among different styles of life. There is a desire for psychological freedom—the freedom to chart one's own course free of open or hidden conditioning pressures. There is a desire for religious freedom—the freedom to search out God in one's own way, and, if no God can be found, the freedom to live a life which has no transcendent being at its center. So put, there are fewer and fewer men in our world who would dissent from this consensus.

Yet it is not enough for modern man that this freedom be theoretically available; not enough that his nation boast a beautifully conceived constitution guaranteeing his rights; not enough that his church have a theology which vindicates his freedom of conscience; not enough that the savants deplore undue social, economic, and cultural coercion. What matters is that man's freedom be real, concrete, and effective, a freedom which can be exercised openly, safely, and fully. The Negro in America has constitutional freedoms, but he often does not yet have real freedom. The religious believer in the Soviet Union has legally guaranteed rights, but he cannot freely exercise these rights without paying a penalty. The poverty stricken slum dweller in Latin America has the social right to economic mobility and a decent life, but those who control the wealth do not give him the opportunity to realize this right. If modern man is a skeptic, he is especially distrustful of paper values, good only for looking and not for acting.

The contemporary world has been a hard school. About man's freedom it has taught him to beware of absolutes, whether these absolutes be ideological, spiritual, moral, or political. Above all it has taught him to be excessively wary of giving his wholehearted allegiance to any scheme of values which entails that he sacrifice his independence, his freedom of choice and judgment. Politically, he has learned that his freedom is safe only where the power of government is relative, subject to checks and balances, limited in scope and application. Ideologically, he has learned that there exists no cause which is more valuable than the good of persons; men do not exist to be sacrificed for abstractions, even if labelled "humanity." Morally, he has learned that ethical values often reflect nothing more than regional traditions, tribal customs, the mores of ruling elites, or the vestigial habits of dead generations. Theologically, he has learned that men often make God in their own image, domesticating religion so that it may better serve, justify, and rationalize the status quo of society.

So much then for the lessons of the contemporary world. To the extent that the Catholic lives in this world and breathes its air, he will have been tutored along with all other men. Perhaps it is true that this education has been mainly negative, telling him more what to avoid than what to seek. Perhaps it is true that, in an age when old certainties are losing their savor, man is left without mooring, turned back in upon himself and doomed to seek an elusive selfhood. Perhaps so, but he cannot for all that ignore what he has learned.

Now let us turn to that world which the Church represents, that other spiritual space in which the layman exists. For one who has taken seriously the lessons of the secular world, the contrast is striking. Here is an institution which, it is commonly believed, demands of its members absolute submission, absolute commitment; hence it rejects that secular wisdom which warns that loyalties should always be provisional. Here is an organization which has at its head a human being of whom the astounding claim is made that, on occasion, he is absolutely protected from error; hence it ignores the advice to be wary of any leader whose followers argue that he is one set apart from ordinary, finite humanity. Here is a community of men which, in its manuals, proclaims the freedom of man's conscience, but which in the past has been known to advocate the burning of dissidents and even now is perfectly willing to banish the heretic into the outer darkness; hence it exhibits one important characteristic of those totalitarian states with an official party line. Here is a social structure which, far from having a system of checks and balances, centers power in the hands of a few men only, men not chosen for their office by those whom they command, and men from whose decisions there is no higher recourse; hence it ignores the experience of a humanity which has suffered at the hands of sovereign lords and dictators.

This list need not be continued. Its thrust should be clear. What are we to say at this point? We could say that what is true in the world is not true in the Church, that what is valuable wisdom for man in his political life does not apply in the Church. This will not do. The Church has always been able to profit from the conclusions of reasonable men meditating on human existence; it should be able to profit in this instance. Nor can we be so naive as to think that the ills which afflict the secular world cannot afflict the Church. The Church is made up of men and it will show the marks of their humanity. Or we could say that the world is correct in its hard-won truths about freedom, but that the Church is so unique an institution that these truths can safely be ignored. Here we might say: Yes, let man be wary of those who claim to have a special access to truth; but let him make an exception in the case of the Church's claims. Yes, let men reject systems of government which contain no checks and balances on the exercise of power; but let them accept the absolute power of the Church, for in that exceptional instance the authority to command obedience comes directly from God. Yes, let no man form his conscience according to the commands of others or suspend his right to absolute moral choice—except in that unique case where the Church teaches one what to choose. These stratagems will not do either.

The difference between the Church and a totalitarian government cannot simply turn on the fact that the former preaches the truth and the latter falsehood. It cannot turn on an assertion that a person should hold on to his freedom when a dictator would take it from him, but should give it up if the Church bids him to do so. It cannot turn on a claim to freedom of choice in the face of a monolithic society, but allow a relinquishment of that freedom when the monolith happens to be a church.

The difference between the Church and an absolutist system of political power must be so sharp there can be no question of making "distinctions" of that kind. In recent decades, much has been done and said to allay the fear of non-Catholics that the Church is essentially a many-tentacled, power-hungry monster. Yet it has by no means convinced the world that the values it appears to represent in the province of authority—absolute commitment to absolute truth mediated by men with absolute power—are compatible with freedom and human dignity. Those who exercise authority may be benevolent, enlightened, sensitive, humble, self-effacing. For all that, and even granting the many limitations on ecclesiastical authority which Catholic theology recognizes, there appears to remain a residue of absolutism. And absolutism, whatever the form it may take, represents a potential danger to freedom, a danger verified by history time and again. At the moment the world looks upon the Church as an ally; now the Church stands with the freedom of man. But it has not always done so in the past. As for the future—who can tell? That is why the Church remains an object of suspicion.

Despite the Council's affirmation of religious liberty and freedom of conscience, the wariness and suspicion will remain. For, from the viewpoint of the world, the Church still claims a special access to truth and a special mandate to proclaim that truth in a binding way. For all the world can see, there is nothing in logic or history which would make it impossible for a future Council to overturn the work of the present Council; or for future popes to declare that the work of our contemporary popes was a mistake. If Catholic thought can change once on religious liberty it can change again. The Catholic may protest here, asserting with full sincerity that the Church will not regress. But he cannot prove it, and he surely is not prophetic enough to speak with absolute confidence about the possible pronouncements of a Council or pope one, two, or three centuries from now. The world thinks it sees absolutism, and it has learned to its great cost that with absolutism all things are possible.

Enough has been said here to indicate a problem of considerable magnitude. A number of questions arise. Is it true, as the world is now coming to hold, that any institution or system of thought which contains an element of absolutism constitutes a potential danger to freedom? If this is so, does that word "any" actually include *even* the Church? Is it further true that any man who by an act of faith commits himself totally and irrevocably to a system of values, an institution, or a church, is no longer a free man? (It will not do here to quickly answer that as long as his absolute commitment was a matter of free choice no problem of freedom need arise. Many men joined the SS of their own free choice.) Is it true that the sensible man, one who has learned the lessons of history well, is a person skeptical of all absolute values, absolute authorities, absolute truths? If this is true, does that mean that the Catholic is, by definition, one who is not wise? I will not try to answer these questions directly, for I doubt that such is what the situation demands. Any Catholic with a minimal training in philosophy and theology could unearth some old sayings or propositions to handle them; but that method has been tried and found wanting.

Let me instead suggest that the Church must try to give the

world not only nicely reasoned theological positions, but also a new *experience*, by word and deed, of the compatibility of freedom and commitment, of freedom and strong authority, of freedom and the acceptance of values which do not spring wholly from human creativity. The Christian must always affirm that an acceptance of Christ can only be a total acceptance. It cannot be provisional or tentative; if it is, it is not faith of the kind Christ asked of men. Morcover, the Catholic must hold that the acceptance of the authority of the Church is inextricably bound up with his faith in Christ; and this means accepting the authority of those who speak in Christ's name. Finally, commitment to Christ and His Church means that one accepts the revelation of Christ's life, death, and resurrection, and the values, stemming wholly from God, which the event of that revelation carries with it. In the face of the wisdom of the world, however, it is no good just to assert these convictions, much less to claim that no danger to freedom arises. The world must, somehow, *see* for itself. It must observe with its own eyes the fact of Catholics acting freely, experiencing freedom, standing forth as witnesses to freedom.

The reason why the Church must enable men to see freedom does not entirely turn upon the necessary apostolic goal of drawing all men to Christ. It also turns upon the need of the world for positive examples, creative insights, and workable suggestions which would assist it in resolving some of its own purely temporal dilemmas, especially those concerning the relationship of one human being with another. I have mentioned that mankind has become skeptical of absolutist political systems, moral and spiritual values. While this is, I think, a valid observation, one can also note that few men are happy living in a universe which requires unremitting cynicism and skepticism. Human beings want values; they want goals toward which they can strive. They have learned to be suspicious of those men and groups proclaiming that they alone possess the truth, but they still show every sign of wanting to find the truth. In civic life, enlightened men do not want dictatorships or military rule; but they do want firm, positive reasons for obeying legitimate laws. In education, students less and less want autocratic teachers presenting them with ready-made wisdom; but they do want to believe there remains the possibility of becoming wise. In ethics, men no longer want detailed lists of moral injunctions; but they do want some sense that moral values have an intrinsic meaning and man's dignity some transcendent significance.

All of this is only to say that the world is confused. It has learned some of its lessons well, and conclusions have been drawn. Yet it has not learned where to go from here. That is why the freedom of the layman has a special importance: as a test case of whether there exists the possibility of a total commitment which remains fully compatible with human freedom. If there does exist such a possibility, to be found in a commitment to Christ and His Church, then it ought to be possible to realize man's freedom in the Christian life. The alternative is ominous. If freedom cannot be realized in the Christian life, a life grounded on the profound conviction that man is made in the image of God, then it is hard to see how it can be realized anywhere else. Much, then, is at stake in the way the Church comes to work out the freedom of the layman: a viable example for the world, the Church's effectiveness in witnessing to the freedom of the children of God, and the possibility of the efficacious presence of the Church among men.

Before suggesting how the Church might demonstrate, in the life of the layman, the possibility of freedom joined with commitment, let me confess to a considerable uneasiness. I do not have a clear vision of a perfect resolution of the apparently conflicting demands posed by the world's perception of the conditions required for freedom and the Church's call to faith and obedience. Like many another lay Catholic, I suspect, I see the persuasiveness of each claim; but the precise key to their ultimate reconciliation escapes me. Yet to say as much will, I hope, help to break the ice. If the layman is to make any contribution in working out these complicated puzzles, a good place to start is by admitting the gaps in his perception.

Nonetheless, there are many pointers toward a reconciliation available in the Church of Vatican II. Taken together they may be able to provide the ingredients of a solution.

1. The most important advance of the contemporary Church lies in the dawning recognition that Christianity has as its sole end and meaning the encounter of the human person with the person of Christ; and through Christ, in the Spirit, with God the Father. This point need not be elaborated here. It will suffice only to note that this recognition shifts the emphasis of the Christian life away from a law-centered, individualistic spirituality to a spirituality of personal growth in holiness realized in and through the human community. Law is not denied. Instead, it is put into a new perspective. Most importantly, the layman is put in a better position to understand the uniqueness of his relationship with God—to understand, that is, how radically different love of God and His Church is from loyalty to a temporal ruler and a secular institution.

2. This uniqueness is emphasized by a fresh awareness of the work of the Holy Spirit in the life of the individual. I think it fair to say that, at least in the recent past, the layman believed the Holy Spirit could move him only through the mediation of the teaching authority of the Church. In short, what did not proceed from authority, or did not have the explicit sanction of authority, was thought worthy of suspicion: the perfect layman did not initiate, he only followed. Today, by contrast, we are coming to see that the Holy Spirit can work through the individual layman, not only on occasion by leading him to enlighten or rebuke authority, but also by impelling him to act freely on his own initiative in the service of Christ. The Spirit is present in the whole Church, that is, in each person in the Church.

3. The whole Church is the People of God. That means the Church is a community, made up of people each with different gifts, vocations, and functions, but each sharing a common humanity, equality, and destiny in the eyes of God. Some will have the power of orders (priests); some will have the power of jurisdiction (bishops and popes); some will have neither of these powers (the laity). Nonetheless, these different functions do not disturb the Christian equality of each person; and that is a significant basis for personal freedom. Even amidst a hierarchial order, Christian equality implies a fraternal relationship of those teaching

and those taught, of ruler and ruled. Those who rule can only do so by serving, and the spirit of service will be demonstrated by humility and openness.

4. Humility and openness, however, should spring from motives fuller than the spirit of childlike simplicity which should be the mark of all Christians. For one who holds authority there should be a deep appreciation of the inescapable fact that only God is our Lord. The authority of a pope, of a bishop, is only a relative authority, given by God, subject to God. In theory there is no difficulty here, but practice is another matter. The Church has always been subject to the temptations of the world, and nowhere has this been more evident than in the tendency of ecclesiastical authority to effect the manner and airs of the secular ruler (and, by and large, the people have approved). Perhaps now the Church is coming to see that, however understandable this tendency, it ill befits an authority whose very presence must symbolize a total submission to God. But this is all of a piece with perceiving that authority in the Church can neither be likened to, nor should it emulate, any other system of authority in the world.

5. It is that latter perception which, little by little, is coming to reshape Catholic education. The shrewd secular ruler has long known that conditioned responses are supremely useful tools for shaping a docile and uncritically loyal populace. The Church, to put it gently, has not always disdained a use of these tools. An emphasis on conformity to Church law, a rigorous system of school and Church discipline, a dependence on external sanctions, a triumphalistic reciting of institutional glories, a suspicion of the original mind, a suppression of dissenters, a doting upon letter-perfect orthodoxy, a will-centered morality, a glorification of the submissive personality—all of these have been characteristic of much Catholic life and thought. Today they are slowly being rejected, though the changing of catechetical and juridical methods is by no means an easy matter.

6. Of no slight importance here is the revolution which has taken place in the Church's understanding of religious liberty. By and large, the great conciliar and pre-conciliar debates on

religious liberty turned on the problem of the religious liberty of non-Catholics. This was only natural. The rise of the pluralistic state and the favored place of democratic forms of government combined with a widespread legal separation of Church and State brought the nineteenth-century position of the Church under heavy fire. No longer does the Church talk the language of "thesis-hypothesis." No longer does one hear that "error has no rights" (a meaningless expression, anyway). Instead, the liberty of all men to seek God and to worship Him in their own way is proclaimed—or not to seek Him and not to worship Him.

But one can hardly discuss the liberty of non-Catholics without, by implication, saying something about the religious liberty of Catholics. For if the non-Catholic must be allowed to follow his conscience, then so surely must the Catholic. That means the conscience of the Catholic dissenter, even of the apostate and the heretic, must be respected. Though this implication of a full understanding of religious liberty is still rarely discussed, it looms on the horizon. That the Church has been slow of late in condemning doctrinal aberrations, willing to tolerate bold new lines of theological speculation, and reluctant to resort to excommunication, suggests that practice is now well ahead of theory. The result one might hope for in this direction is the minimizing of impossible choices; that is, situations in which the Catholic believes himself forced to choose between suppressing honest doubts about this or that article of the faith (and thus being dishonest with himself and others) and leaving the Church.

7. These relatively abstract pointers toward freedom need to be complemented by some specific institutions designed to promote and insure freedom. There is considerable merit in the numerous suggestions for giving laymen a legally established and guaranteed right to be heard in the Church. It is of no use assuring the layman that his voice counts if there is no way in which it can be heard and no obligation on the part of authority to listen. The development of a body of lay theologians, the presence of laymen in diocesan synods, in Roman offices, on conciliar commissions, in administrative positions in Catholic education—the

list of possibilities is endless—will insure a hearing for lay opinion. To this list should be added a canonically guaranteed right to petition (easily) for the redress of grievances, the right to full information on Church finances and procedures, the right of public protest against abuses of authority—again, the possibilities are infinite.

One might aptly observe at this point that the laity already have a considerable voice and influence. Despite some grumbling, the recent outbursts of lay criticisms and suggestions have been tolerated, even encouraged; there have been no significant reprisals, no monitums, no silencings. Moreover, the conciliar debates gave every indication that the Bishops are not incapable of listening, and responding to the laity. But it is important to bear in mind that all of this progress has been achieved more or less by accident; or, better, one would like to say, through the unexpected workings of the Holy Spirit. There is nothing yet in the *structure* of the Church which provides for the guaranteed continuation of this permissiveness, this creative listening on the part of the hierarchy, which we are now experiencing. Little imagination is required to envision the possibility of another generation of popes and bishops deciding that the laity ought, once again, to be seen and not heard. There is nothing in the juridical workings of the Church to prevent such a reversal, nor much at this point that the laity could do to stop it. That possibility entails the necessity of written rights and guarantees. The freedom of the laity should never again be dependent upon the mood of an historical moment, or upon the charitable toleration of those who rule. As the Chinese know, those who have the unilateral power to magnanimously allow one hundred flowers to bloom also have the power to uproot them.

These seven pointers (and one might list others) seem to me to provide the main elements of a solution to the dilemma of freedom and authority. If they can be put together, then one word I used earlier should no longer have any meaningful sense with reference to the Church: the word "absolute." At the present time, it still remains possible to talk of *absolute* power in the

Church. But the word ought to have an alien ring to the Christian; and if the Christian manages to be what he should be, then it should seem to all men an inappropriate word to use when speaking of one who follows Christ.

How could men ever describe as absolutists those who commit themselves to Christ as free men giving themselves to Him who loves them? Or those who freely belong to a community radically rooted in human dignity and equality? Or those who believe that the Spirit can blow where it will, directly illuminating even the least gifted among us? Or those who reject with a passion the manipulating of the mind and the conditioning of the emotions? Or those for whom the dissenter is not the enemy but rather the suffering brother or the prophetic brother? Or those who look upon religious liberty as a sacred right, to be taken from no man? Or those who, in their institutions and legal structures, have provided clear safeguards against the abuse of authority? Or those who, whatever their position, never forget that all they have comes from God?

Let me put aside theological definitions of the laymen. Let me, instead, call him Everyman. He is the man who, in political society, is only a statistic, his person all but invisible to the naked eye, the victim of forces he cannot control, leaders he cannot influence, and a history he did not make. The critical problem of our age of the mass society is to recognize his existence, to give flesh and blood and freedom to him as a person. One would like to say the problem is totally different within the Church, but it is not. That is why the achieving of freedom for the layman in the Church could have a meaning which goes well beyond the Church. For if it is not possible for a Christian to be free in a community of Christians, then it is unlikely that any man will for long be free in any kind of community. What is it for a man to be free? Now we have to answer that question with words. Someday, perhaps, we will be able to answer it merely by picking out a layman at random and pointing to him. Words are not needed when the eye can see.

CHAPTER TEN

What Has the Council Made of the Layman?

NEARLY A DECADE AGO, FATHER YVES CONGAR WROTE IN HIS pioneering book *Lay People in the Church* that a fresh theology of the laity required, first of all, a fresh theology of the Church. He could hardly have been more accurate. Despite the vast mass of writing and talking about the laity, it is still hard to see many concrete results in the actual life of the Church. To be sure, there are now some laymen on a few scattered school boards and ecumenical commissions; here and there plans are being laid for diocesan councils with lay participation; a few laymen took an active role in Vatican II. Yet these are surely meager results: a good start, but not much more. Perhaps, just perhaps, there are proportionately more laymen actively trying to give witness in their secular work. Who knows?

The trouble all along has been the apparent impossibility of doing two things at once: giving the layman his head while at the same time preserving the hierarchical structure of the Church.

Father Congar saw this problem clearly. To tack a rich understanding of the layman to a stale, rigid understanding of the Church is a venture doomed from the outset. Something of the kind was tried with the idea of the organized lay apostolate. Pope Pius XII welcomed the layman into the service of the Church, but only on the condition that the layman's work was to be understood as subsidiary to the work of the hierarchical apostolate. There was only the faintest hint that the laymen had a quite independent sacramental basis for his apostolic life: his baptism and confirmation.

The consequences of this oversight were enormous. Only those lay activities which were carefully sanctioned and controlled had any recognized standing at all. That meant the great mass of laymen were untouched; only "joiners" and the docile, those willing to carry out the directions of others, had any real place. As if that were not enough, there were many sour memories of lay trusteeism and fears of lay insubordination still around to dampen any general enthusiasm for a greater lay role. Needless to say, there was much lay grumbling. It took a supreme act of faith to believe that the hierarchy and clergy were really serious about the layman. Maybe they wanted to be, but that could be seen only in their words, not in their deeds.

But was clerical reluctance the only problem? For a time it seemed to be. Change the "attitude" of the clergy and the bishops! Change the seminary curriculum to emphasize the layman's dignity! Open up channels of communication between clergy and laity! These were some of the panaceas offered; they all presupposed that some tinkering with the system would eradicate the problem. Good will and mutual understanding would save the day!

We know better now. On the one hand, it turned out that many apparently rigid priests were themselves chafing at the bit. They wanted to give the layman his rightful place, but could not gain permission from their bishop to do so. They were caught up in the system just as much as the layman, though this was not always apparent. On the other hand, many bishops were equally stymied. They had few precedents, little canonical sanction, and many older, worried pastors standing in their way. The bishops could (so many felt) do only what tradition allowed them to; priests could do only what their bishops allowed; and laymen could only do what priests allowed. In brief, it was a perfect vicious circle, far more than good will and tinkering could cope with.

How is this circle to be broken? Of course it still exists, despite all our brave and noble words about the layman. At first glance, chapter 4 of the *Constitution on the Church* (surely one of the most important documents of Vatican II) appears to provide an answer. That chapter, given over to the laity, does indeed include many valuable steps forward. It points out that the bishops "were not ordained by Christ to take upon themselves alone the entire salvific mission of the Church toward the world." It points out that all Christians, regardless of rank or ministry, share a common dignity stemming from "One Lord, one faith, one baptism." It points out that the laity have "the noble duty of working to extend the divine plan of salvation to all men of each epoch and in every land." It points out that the laity share in Christ's "priestly function of offering spiritual worship for the glory of God and salvation of man." It points out that Christ fulfills his prophetic office, not only through the hierarchy, "but also through the laity whom he made his witnesses and to whom he gave understanding of the faith (*sensu fidei*). . . ."

So far so good. There is nothing in these words which could possibly justify taking the layman as anything less than a full member of the Church. There is nothing to justify the assumption that the layman's apostolic, priestly, and prophetic role is of an inferior kind. And there is even more. The bishops are exhorted to "recognize and promote the dignity as well as the responsibility of the laity in the Church. Let them confidently assign duties to them in the service of the Church, allowing them freedom and room for action. . . . Attentively in Christ, let them consider with fatherly love the projects, suggestions and desires proposed by the laity . . . let the shepherds respectively acknowledge that just

freedom which belongs to everyone in this earthly city." Moreover, the laity are "by reason of the knowledge, competence or
outstanding ability which they may enjoy, permitted and sometimes even obliged to express their opinions on those things which
concern the good of the Church."

Could one ask for anything more? Is there not in these passages the breakthrough long sought? Well, yes and no. Yes: to
the extent that the layman has now been given full backing when
he feels compelled to speak out in the Church. Yes: to the extent
that bishops are urged to heed lay opinions and suggestions. Yes:
to the extent that laymen must have freedom of initiative to
carry out their work.

But there is also room to say *no* here. For instance, just after
the passage in which the laity are given the right to speak, there
is the following sentence: "When occasions arise, let this be done
through the organs erected by the Church for this purpose." In
other words, speak: but only through channels, only in officially
approved and structured ways, only by those means authoritatively
sanctioned. No, then: to the extent that no provision is made for
public appeals to the whole Church, or directly to a bishop or
pope. And, anyway, where are these "organs"? The passage reads
as if they already exist.

They do not, and one searches in vain for any instructions
to bishops to begin establishing them. Judging from the minimal
efforts being made, one can only conclude that the bishops do not
believe the Constitution in any way actually compels or orders
them to do so. Once again, then, the vicious circle: the layman
may speak if he does so through established organs, but the
bishops are not required to erect such organs (nor, presumably,
are pastors).

I trust this comment will not be taken just as another piece
of carping lay criticism; as if, no matter what is said and done by
the Council, the layman will never be satisfied. The important
thing to see is that, unless the noble words and strong exhortations
are carried through into concrete structures and changes, long-
standing inertia will continue to rule. The weight of centuries is

behind the vicious circle; it will not be broken by anything less than decisive and dramatic changes.

Is there any way out, granting that chapter 4 of the *Constitution* does not quite manage to find it? From one point of view the problem appears absolutely intractable. If one starts from the hierarchial structure of the Church, the need to maintain an orderly exercise of papal and episcopal authority, then it is extraordinarily difficult to see how the Church could ever really give the layman effective freedom and influence. It is as if, to choose a bizarre possibility, the American people suddenly decided they wanted an absolute monarch, but at the same time wanted to retain the present American Constitution in its full rigor. The combination could not be managed; absolute monarchies and constitutional democracies are logically and practically incompatible.

Yet we seem to be trying to unite equally irreconcilable concepts in the Church: absolute hierarchical authority and a free, responsible laity. Maybe there is an ingenious solution possible here, but I have not seen it. They all end at one or the other of two extremes. The libertarian extreme emphasizes the solidly grounded theological truth that the layman must follow his conscience even if this means a separation from the Church. The authoritarian extreme, no less solidly grounded, would affirm with the *Constitution on the Church* that "The laity should, as all Christians, promptly accept in Christian obedience decisions of their spiritual shepherds." But what of the person who cannot bring himself in conscience to give obedience in a particular instance, yet does not want to leave the Church either? No one knows what to do with *him*. There is no place in a Church conceived in hierarchical, authoritarian terms for this person at all. Nor is there, to choose a less drastic case, a place for the layman who wants to carry through some apostolic work for which he cannot gain ecclesiastical approval. He can go ahead hoping that the axe will not fall (and often enough, in practice, it does not), but in a showdown he may well be faced with the choice of obeying authority or leaving the Church. Again, the vicious circle.

Fortunately, there is another point of view available, though so far it lacks full development. It can be found both explicitly and implicitly in the first two chapters of the *Constitution*. For it is in those chapters that we are given a vision of the Church as a mystery, as a community, as the People of God. These rich, scriptural concepts have been much discussed and there is no need for me to elaborate on them here. Taken together, however, they succeed in decisively shifting an emphasis from the Church as a structured hierarchical society to the Church as a living community of men, each bound to the service of the other and all committed to the service of God. Naturally, these chapters do not scorn or ignore the special charisms of the popes and bishops. There are such gifts and they must be taken seriously. But they are not dwelt on; there is not the kind of nervous obsession with them which sets in with the third chapter of the *Constitution*, ponderously titled "On the Hierarchical Structure of the Church and in Particular on the Episcopate."

The most striking thing about the first two chapters of the *Constitution* is that they do not approach the Church as many of the older manuals were prone to do. The manuals often began by defining the Church as a "society," a perfect society, and then went on to emphasize the need for authority in that society (as in any other society). From there, everyone was then given his slot, his place on the great hierarchical ladder. This approach was eminently tidy, as tidy, unfortunately, as the most rigid and monolithic political societies (which was hardly surprising since they supplied the basic model).

That is not the approach of the first two chapters of the *Constitution*. The very first note struck is that of the Church as a mystery. The Church is "the kingdom of Christ now present in mystery." Yet this kingdom is capable of growth; it is not a static, but a dynamic mystery. Should the Church ever stand still, it would be denying itself. Christ it was who inaugurated this kingdom and who revealed to us its mystery. When the work of Christ on earth was completed, the Holy Spirit was sent "in order that He might continually sanctify the Church." Not only does the

Holy Spirit dwell in the Church, "He both equips and directs with hierarchical and charismatic gifts and adorns with his fruits." Note the expression "hierarchical and charismatic gifts"—no one group in the Church has a monopoly on the gifts of the Holy Spirit.

The second great theme of the *Constitution* is that the Church is the "people of God." "God," the *Constitution* points out, "does not make men holy and save them merely as individuals, without bond or link between one another. Rather it has pleased Him to bring men together as one people, a people which acknowledges Him in truth and serves Him in holiness." Thus we are all joined together regardless of rank or ministry. But who are these people and what is their condition? The *Constitution* is direct here: "The state of this people is that of the dignity and freedom of the sons of God, in whose heart the Holy Spirit dwells as in His temple." Not robots or ciphers or conformists, but free men.

To be sure, the *Constitution* does not altogether ignore the importance of the Church as a society. One can see in the third chapter of the *Constitution* that there is no intention of slighting the hierarchical nature of the Church. But it can hardly be denied that the initial and basic thrust is to provide the Church with the biblical and theological insights necessary to envision the Church as a genuine and full community, a community of free persons, joined by a basic Christian equality and common destiny. More than that, the *Constitution* makes clear that the people of God, those who make up the Church, share in Christ's prophetic office. Very strikingly, the Council fathers locate infallibility first of all in the whole Church. As they say, "The entire body of the faithful, annointed as they are by the Holy One, cannot err in matters of belief." It is the whole Church which discerns and preserves the truth. The function of authority is to guide the exercise of this discernment. It is by no means authority alone which can discover truth; on the contrary, its role is mainly to guide and protect what the *whole* Church discerns. In one brief passage, then, the fathers did much to stifle "hierarchology."

It did still more, emphasizing that the Holy Spirit brings his gifts to every individual in the Church. As the fathers expressed it, "He (the Holy Spirit) distributes special graces among the faithful of every rank. By these gifts he makes them fit and ready to undertake the various tasks and offices which contribute toward the renewal and building up of the Church, according to the words of the Apostle: 'The manifestation of the Spirit is given to everyone for profit.' "

Two important consequences follow here. Since infallibility resides in the whole Church (subject to the guidance of the magisterium), the witness and testimony of the laity can never be slighted. Further, since the Holy Spirit gives His gifts to everyone in the Church, no one member, whatever his rank or station, can afford to neglect the possibility that the Holy Spirit may be working here and now through another member of the Church— whatever his rank and station. To put it more directly, no priest, bishop, or pope can ignore the possibility that the Holy Spirit may choose to speak to him—and perhaps the whole Church—through the voice of the lowliest layman.

In this context, the concept of the "priesthood of the faithful" takes on a special prominence. How are we to understand this expression, once considered thoroughly "Protestant"? We can only understand it by going first to the Old Testament. There we read in Exodus 19: 5-6 what Yahweh said to Moses: "Therefore, if you hearken to My voice and keep My Covenant, you shall be my special possession, dearer to Me than all other people, though all the earth is Mine. You shall be to Me a kingdom of priests, a holy nation." God was saying, in brief, that the whole people was empowered and commissioned to acknowledge God, and to offer to Him a sacrifice of praise and honor. This was not to deny a special ministerial priesthood, but it was to point out that there also existed a priesthood of the whole people. Isaiah repeats this theme when he says to the people, "You yourselves shall be named priests of the Lord; ministers of our God you shall be called" (Isaiah 61:6).

This was not a calling of the people which died with the old dispensation. Instead it was amplified by a famous passage in

1 Peter 2: 4–5, 9: "Draw near to Him, a living stone, rejected by men but chosen and honored by God. Be you yourselves as living stone, built thereon into a spiritual house, a royal priesthood, to offer spiritual sacrifices acceptable to God through Jesus Christ. . . . You are a chosen race, a royal priesthood, a holy nation, a purchased people; that you may proclaim the perfections of Him who has called you out of darkness into His marvelous light."

Every Christian is, then, a priest. Each shares in that which is common to every priesthood, the capacity to offer sacrifice to God. That is what is meant by the expression "priesthood of the faithful." Christ it is who is the high priest. He himself offered the highest sacrifice to God—He offered Himself. Each of us shares in His offering. Each of us shares in His priesthood. By virtue of baptism every Christian shares the life and power of Christ.

Naturally, the priesthood of the faithful differs in some important respects from the hierarchical or ministerial priesthood. As the Council fathers put it in the Constitution on the Church: "Though they differ from one another in essence and not only in degree, the common priesthood of the faithful and the ministerial or hierarchical priesthood are nonetheless interrelated: each of them in its own special way is a participation in the one priesthood of Christ. The ministerial priest, by the sacred power he enjoys, teaches and rules the priestly people: acting in the person of Christ, he makes present the eucharistic sacrifice, and offers it to God in the name of all the people. But the faithful, in virtue of their royal priesthood, join in the offering of the Eucharist. They likewise exercise that priesthood in receiving the sacraments, in prayer and thanksgiving, in the witness of a holy life, and by self-denial and active charity."

Here then, at just that place where the layman is thought to be most distinct from the priest, it turns out that they are actually sharers of a common gift, however differently they partake of this gift. St. Augustine has expressed it beautifully: "Just as we call them all christ (i.e., anointed) because of the mystical chrism, we also all are priests by virtue of the fact that they are members of one priest."

It should be wholly unnecessary at this point to assert that the layman is a full member of the Church. Nor should it be necessary to spell out any further how the layman and the priest are intimately joined with each other. The Church is a whole, a people, a community, a body, a society—each phrase has its uses—and every member of the Church must be one with every other member. We are all kings, we are all priests, we are all prophets. And we are all human beings, no one of us complete unto himself, no one of us able to achieve our salvation apart from life with others.

The centrality of the layman in the work and mission of the Church should be starkly clear. Both the *Constitution on the Church* and the *Decree on the Lay Apostolate* break down any overly sharp distinction between the layman's place "in the world" and "in the Church." The layman, his voice, talents, and powers, have a place in the Church and in the world. That said, it remains true that the special province of the layman is the world. Christ, it must constantly be recalled, did not come to man just to save individual souls; he came to save all men, to save them as a people. The spreading of the kingdom, the making universal of this efficacious salvation, depends more than we realize on the willingness and capacity of the laity to transcend their personal spiritual needs. To transcend these needs, not by denying they exist, but by seeing that salvation requires action as well as meditation, witness as well as prayer, sharing as well as storing, spreading as well as gathering.

The layman's eye must be directed outwardly as well as inwardly. What he will see if he is not blind is a world desperately in need of Christ. He will see a world which suffers the ravages of war. He will see a world torn by racial hatreds. He will see a world in which half the population does not get enough to eat. He will see Harlem. He will see Southeast Asia. He will see poverty and unemployment, illiteracy and ignorance. But one need not be so dramatic. He will see well-fed, well-housed, physically comfortable people living shallow, empty lives in drably identical suburban houses. He will see people caught in the rat race of success. He will see lonely old people. He will see neglected, forgotten children. He will see, that is, all the evil and suffering and pain which are the lot of mankind.

That is why the layman must spread the kingdom of the Lord. That is why he must announce the good news. He must bring to this mankind, in the words of the Constitution, "a kingdom of truth and life, a kingdom of holiness and grace, a kingdom of justice, love and peace." That is what the kingdom of God is all about.

With all this in mind, is it now possible to say that the first two chapters of the *Constitution on the Church* succeed in breaking the vicious circle mentioned earlier? That is hard to say with any certainty; at least they look as if they do. They grant and expand upon the various gifts of the Holy Spirit to each member of the Church. And in doing so they do not dwell with excessive force upon the necessity that authority alone be capable of judging the manifestations of these gifts. Most importantly, they give the hierarchical nature of the Church a relatively subordinate position. Hierarchy is not what is important about the Church; hierarchy is not at the heart of the Church; hierarchy is not what characterizes the Church's presence in the world. For this reason, these two chapters have much more to say about the laity (though the word is hardly used) than does the chapter explicitly given to the subject.

A good place to focus and test these insights is the parish. Each layman belongs to a parish, and a parish is both in the Church and the world. No institution is, moreover, in greater need of reform. As in most things Catholic, the greatest obstacles to reforming the parish are human rather than theological. In principle, there is practically nothing standing in the way of a total change in parish life. All that is required to constitute a parish is that there be a minister and that there be people, a ministry, and a community. Beyond that, almost anything is conceivable and possible. The parish we know today is no more than a product of history, convenience, shifting traditions, and canon law. To take an extreme case, there is nothing in Revelation which would oppose the decision of a pope to destroy every existing church building in the world and to order that, henceforth, priests should minister to the people exclusively in their homes or places of work.

Such a decision might evoke some mutterings, however. Almost any decision about, or change in, the parish structure will. And this for a very good reason: no matter how bad any parish may be, there will be some who will love it. People grow attached to the bad just as much to the good. In changing a parish, one changes what is for many the only spiritual home they know, the home they have lived in, prayed in, made friends in, and very possibly will die in. Not everyone who lives in a Victorian house would care to have a contractor come in and, presto, transform it into something fit for a prize in *Architectural Forum*.

I emphasize these human facts to make a homely point. Whatever the parish should become, it will have to remain the kind of human community in which people will feel comfortable. Not comfortable in some pejorative sense—smug, complacent, and so on—but comfortable in the sense that people will feel at ease there, secure in their relations with others who make up the parish community, at home in the physical surroundings, stimulated by and naturally drawn into the kind of life they find there. I would count as a total failure a parish which introduced every item of reformist zeal but which, at the same time, succeeded in antagonizing all but the reformers. That hasn't happened much so far, but its opposite has prevailed for decades: those who sought sharp reforms remained outsiders. In either case the principle remains the same. Any parish which succeeds in making a large number of people feel isolated is a failure, just as is a parish which does not try to make most people feel a full, active partner in its life. The former is a failure of commission, the latter of omission; the results are much the same.

Both of these failures are characteristic of far too many parishes. Everyone knows the common complaints and I will just list them here: most parishes are too big and too impersonal;

most parishes suffer from poor communication between pastor and people, priests and people; most spend too much of their time worrying about money and facilities; most operate with the burden of lay societies and organizations which have no contemporary significance. If one adds to this charming list the constant mobility of people from one parish to another, the class and educational differences which mark most parishes, and the great variations among priests—well, it is remarkable that the parishes have any vitality at all.

Now I realize that some today believe that the key to a revitalized parish lies in the liturgy. Since the liturgy should be the focal point of the parish community, many argue, create a fine spirit of liturgical worship and then all other good things will naturally follow. Actually, I suspect it will have to be the other way around. The liturgy will only take on meaning for the people, only become the center of their life, after they have first created a viable human community. The easiest thing to do in a parish is to change the liturgy and instruct the people in what it means; the hardest is to create a community. A strong, rich, vital community can survive the worst kind of liturgy; what it cannot survive is the death of itself as a community.

What is the key here? It is not the liturgy. It is not the quality of the singing, sermons, or homilies. It is not the enthusiasm of the laity. It is not the amount of money available, or the extent and beauty of the buildings. Instead, it is the quality of the Christian life which the people and priests share, and this quality will be a direct result of their relationship as human beings. How much do they love each other, rejoice with each other, share each other's burdens? That is the crucial question. A second key, hardly less important than the first, is the quality of the relationship between those within the parish and those outside of it. One measure of the parish as a Christian center is its ability to transcend its own bonds of loyalty, support, and affection and to extend them to all men. All men should be loved the way one loves the members of one's parish. (That statement does not describe a fact; it commends an ideal!)

None of this will happen by itself. Some one person, or some few people will have, initially, to set the parish in motion. Left to their own resources, most people will gravitate toward those like themselves, those of like ethnic, class, or educational background. They will tend to build their Christian relationships upon their natural human cliques. And that provides an important clue to the problem. Somehow a way must be found in the parish to lead people beyond their narrow alliances, to make them see that their relationship as Christians has a greater potential for friendship and affection than does any other bond. This is extraordinarily hard for most people to see. We like our own kind.

In general, there is only one effective way to achieve this broadening of relationships. The people of the parish must be led to a living sense of their responsibility for the parish—that is, for each other. But to give this any substance requires that they talk, argue, and physically and mentally work together. It will be their experience in doing this which will, as much as anything else, cut through their natural differences as human beings. They have to physically and mentally touch each other, and this day in and day out. Specifically, though, something more is required. There must be some few people in the parish who take it upon themselves to bring these richer relationships about, to foster and strengthen them. Some few people, that is, who see what it is all about and who, with a discerning eye and a skill in bringing humans into contact, work to create the conditions under which a Christian community becomes possible.

The most logical and appropriate person is the priest. He is the starting point, for he alone is potentially able at the outset to have the time, range of contacts, and professional skills necessary to tie the human knots. As matters now stand in most parishes, it is hard for him to do so. Whatever his wishes might be, administrative chores take up a preponderance of his time. Papers rather than people are likely to be the center of his attention. This has a doubly disastrous effect. It means that he must be unduly concerned about where power and money lie among his parishioners. His first charge is the parish plant, and it is almost inevitable that he will want to see the parish structured in such a way that it contributes to the upkeep of that plant. The second disastrous effect is on the parishioners themselves. They are soon led to believe that their main utility to the parish stems from the contents of their wallet. They are good either at giving money personally or in contributing their time to those activities—bazaars, cake sales, raffles, and the like—which extract money from others. Of course many complain about this, but still more find it wholly satisfactory. In a commercial society, dedicated to the making and spending of money, nothing is likely to seem more ordinary and wholesome than commercial relationships; throw in the presence and interest of a priest and you have just about everything too many people want.

The only way out here is to recreate totally the role of the priest, and that, in turn, entails recreating the role of the laity. So long as the pastor is solely charged by the bishop with the financial solvency of the parish his interests will necessarily be financial. The obvious solution here is to make the parishioners themselves, or at least a representative group, bear this responsibility. They are the ones who should do the worrying, not the priest. Trusteeism? Probably so, but structured in such a way as to avoid some of the obvious drawbacks of the old trustee system. A second requirement, closely related to the first, is that all administrative chores be delegated to the laity. It is an exceedingly rare parish today where talent cannot be found to keep the books, maintain records, superintend the buildings, and write the checks. Nothing is more extravagantly wasteful of a priest's training and time than to be forced into this kind of work. Nothing so dilutes the laity's sense of responsibility for the parish than the hard fact that they are given no important burdens to bear.

But let us assume that the priest could be relieved of these useless drudgeries. Where should he turn his attention? The first place would be to those groupings which depend heavily upon ethnic and class affinities. His job would be to break them up, or, better, to help them break out of their self-enclosed shells. Most parishes now have only a handful of organizations, and as a rule they are least-common-denominator organizations, lacking any contemporary point or aim, directed toward attracting as many people as possible. As it usually happens, the direction and activities of these organizations fall into the hands of one or another clique; and they take on the tone of that clique.

Here the parish priests become crucial. If they are nervous, and many are, they are prone to like this arrangement; it gives them fewer people to keep their eye on, fewer leaders to deal with. Yet what is really required is a great variety of organizations, built around a great range of interests. The size of the groups does not matter—some may have a hundred, others only a handful. The critical point is whether they represent concerns which have genuine spiritual and human meaning. For this kind of variety to exist requires priests who are willing to relinquish control and direction. They have to be conceived by laymen and run by laymen. The main function of the priest would be something of a gadfly. He would direct parishioners toward certain groups, stimulate them with ideas and insights, and encourage the formation of new groups whenever a need appeared.

On a broader level, he would see to it that all major decisions in the parish represented as broad a consensus as possible. He would unceasingly work to bring more and more people into the decision-making process. This is already being tried in some places, and it is very likely to work. But even if it does not, even if it leads to much confusion, it would still be preferable to the present arrangement which places all authority in the hands of the pastor. What counts is not the efficiency of the parish, the smoothness with which it operates, but the way in which it makes everyone a full partner. That is the essence of community.

I am suggesting, then, two special tasks for the priests and pastor. On the one hand, they should work for a wide range of small groups, each directed toward useful, spiritually profitable work or study. The more of these there are, the less will the pastor and priests have to do with any of them directly. On the other hand, they should also work toward forging all of these individuals and small groups into a broad, decision-making body. For the parishioners themselves, the small groups will provide practical experience in spiritual self-direction; they cannot depend upon priests to guide their steps on specific problems. But as members of the whole parish, they will also learn the value of working out their common destiny as a people. All the while, the priests will constantly move about—prodding this group, instructing that, making suggestions to one, providing insights to another. They will never dominate and rarely will they lead. Their main consideration will be how well and how fruitfully the people become one.

The *Decree on the Apostolate of the Laity*, especially section 10, provides a fine set of goals. Very perceptively it emphasizes that the laity can help and assist each other and, no less significantly, that they can "refresh the spirit of pastors." I like that, for I think very few laymen realize that they have a responsibility to care for the souls of their pastors and priests; they usually think it exclusively the other way around. The Decree also emphasizes that the laity should bring to "the Church community their own and the world's problems as well as questions concerning human salvation, all of which they should examine and resolve by deliberating in common." If I read that phrase "questions concerning human salvation" correctly, I take it the Council fathers were encouraging basic theological discussion in the parish, and saying that even these matters—formerly the sole preserve of professional theologians—are open to common lay deliberation. A very radical and provocative idea, indeed.

Finally, the decree comes down hard on the importance of the parish increasingly extending its scope of interest and responsibility: to the diocesan, the national, and the international level. Most parishes today are grossly provincial. Their only contact with the rest of the Church is by an occasional donation to some national or international collection. But it should be apparent that rich parishes could well adopt small parishes as part of their overall responsibility—and by that I mean take on the debts of other parishes, which is where the bite would be most real. This would require a special kind of sanctity on the part of the priests. They would have to tolerate, even encourage, the weakening of their own parish's financial strength for the sake of other parishes. So, too, they would have to encourage some people to give their money to secular organizations rather than to the parish. They can't be constantly reiterating their own needs, giving them primary attention, and expect the people magically to develop a sense of responsibility beyond the parish.

There have been many complaints of late about the traditional "geographical" parish, and a good case can be made that it is obsolete. But I would argue that it is as good an arrangement as any. It needs to be heavily supplemented by special parishes, professional organizations, and imaginative experiments in finding people where they are, whether on the job, in slums, or at play. Yet the geographical parish has the great advantage of forcing very disparate assortments of people to live, worship, and work together. Perhaps it is utopian to say so, but if the idea of Christian community has any significance at all, it should be able to bring into unity the most different kinds of persons. The geographical parish provides this possibility—depending, of course, on the ability of the priests and people to transcend their human differences, good in themselves, for the sake of something better. If, as sometimes happens, a parish becomes a one-class parish, then a little judicious gerrymandering of parish boundaries can help counteract this. Should that fail, then it may become imperative for parishes in different places to form working alliances with each other: suburban and inner city parishes, for instance, exchanging money, help, people, and counsel.

Whatever happens, though, the test of a Christian parish will be the vitality of its human relationships. Clerical paternalism kills the human. Lay factions kill the human. Liturgy without community kills the human. Excessive building drives kill the human. Money-raising can kill the human. That alone saves the human which brings people into contact with each other, which makes of them a whole, which finds their talents and skills and tries to develop them, which makes each person responsible for every other person. There is not much of this now in the ordinary parish, and it is a shame—both laymen and priest suffer.

Let me sketch a picture of the layman which could be drawn from the Council. He is a person fully conscious that the Holy Spirit can work through him; indeed that the Holy Spirit will give him those gifts necessary to carry out his ministry in the Church and world. He is a person who takes it for granted that he is a co-worker with priests and bishops. He knows that if he has something to say, he can say it—and he will be listened to, for he is treated as an equal. The clergy respect his gifts and talents, rather different from their own, just as he respects theirs. He does not worry about getting permission for this or that initiative. As long as he respects the gifts of others, and their opinions, he can do whatever seems to him necessary.

For his part, this layman pays a special respect to the pope and to the bishops. He knows it is their task and duty to give him broad guidance and to establish some regulatory laws in the Church. But he also knows they would not think of laying down any laws, defining any doctrines, or taking any disciplinary measures without first consulting him (or at least his representative). He knows, of course, that the pope, his bishop, or his pastor may not always be able to follow his suggestions or solve problems in a way which seems sensible to him; but he has a full moral assurance that his opinions are taken seriously and that, more often than not, any authoritative decision will represent a genuine consensus of lay, priestly, and episcopal opinion. He would find it utterly inconceivable that a pastor or a bishop would conduct his pastorate from behind closed doors. He would know the workings of the local parish and the chancery office almost as well as his pastor or bishop. Naturally, this layman would stay well-informed, for at any moment he might be called upon to help the bishop frame a pastoral letter, or deal with a matter of the Church's relationship to society, or be asked to help fashion a parish or diocesan budget. Whenever something of possible value occurred to him, he would feel no hesitation about inviting his pastor or bishop over to dinner, or at least writing a letter. He would be assured of a response; after all, he knows, and those in authority know, that he is a person to be reckoned with.

Now and then, some real conflicts would arise. They always will. Yet when they do, this layman knows that the bishop or his pastor will suffer, just as he will suffer. There will be no curt notes from the chancery office, no formal letters from the bishop, no unanswered phone calls at the rectory. Those in conflict will meet face to face, as human beings, each trying to be faithful to his conscience and his duties, each recoiling in horror from the possibility that their friendship and mutual respect should be broken. If worse comes to worst, they will pray together, bring in others to listen to each side of the dispute. If that fails, then it fails; but everything will have been done that could be done.

Idealistic? Romantic? Unrealistic? Certainly, but then so is Christianity. There is no vicious circle in that picture; instead there is freedom, humanity, openness. There is no less legitimate authority either; instead, there is authority exercised in humility, in charity, in suffering. How long do we have to wait?

CHAPTER ELEVEN

Reforming the Catholic Universtiy

I

BEFORE ATTEMPTING TO GENERALIZE ABOUT THE AMERICAN CATHolic university today and some of its needs let me sketch a brief description of its history and the social context of that history. The first thing to be borne in mind is that during much of the seventeenth and eighteenth centuries American Catholics were proscribed by law from holding public office, from voting and from opening Catholic schools of any kind. Nor were they, so far as I am able to determine, free to attend Harvard, Yale, or Princeton. Those colleges were all established under Protestant auspices, their main purpose being the training of Protestant ministers. Thus any of those early Anglo-American Catholics who desired an advanced education had to go abroad—usually to France. By the time of the American Revolution, however, the climate had changed. If Catholics were still suspect to many of

124

their Protestant neighbors, they at least soon gained full legal and political rights. Their loyalty during the Revolution helped, moreover, to make them socially acceptable, as did the fact that they shared a common language and a common ancestry with most Protestants. But they still remained a distinct and small minority and, with the exception of a few small Catholic academies established in the late eighteenth century, they had no educational facilities of their own. Of particular importance, the non-Catholic colleges still remained, in practice, closed to them.

From the very first, then, the early clergy and bishops were faced with an urgent problem. If the faith of the Catholic was to be preserved and strengthened, then education was of primary importance. Since non-Catholics were unwilling to make their schools acceptable to Catholics, there seemed no choice but for Catholics to create their own institutions. Toward this end, the first bishop, John Carroll, made Catholic education one of his main concerns. Among the very first steps he took was the establishment of Georgetown Academy, outside Washington, in 1789. That Academy, which was soon taken over by the Jesuits, became the first American Catholic college. Thereafter, American Catholic education slowly increased in scope and strength. While priority was given to grammar schools, there was a gradual increase in the number of colleges throughout the nineteeth century, and their number continued to grow during the first half of the twentieth century.

In the course of the nineteenth century, however, much of the social acceptance which the Anglo-American Catholics had been able to achieve for Catholicism just before and just after the Revolution was lost with the influx of the great waves of Irish immigrants who began arriving after the 1830s. Most of the blame for this change must be laid at the feet of the established Protestant majority who rejected the immigrants as much out of resentment and fear of their "foreign" ways as out of a distaste for their religion. As the century progressed, Catholics tended to turn inward upon themselves, to become defensive and insular. Not all of them were this way, but enough were to cut Catholicism off from the mainstream of American intellectual and cultural life. Ghettoism, whether in a real or a figurative sense, reigned supreme. If this was understandable and a common reaction of rejected minorities in any society, it was still very damaging to Catholics themselves.

It was certainly damaging in the sphere of Catholic higher education. For it meant that the Catholic colleges were looked upon as much to protect the student's faith and morals from the dangers of society as they were to provide a solid education. In addition, the faculties of these colleges had comparatively little contact with the faculties of non-Catholic colleges. Slowly but surely, the Catholic intellectual world became a self-sufficient one. As if to confirm its self-sufficiency, there began to appear in the 1920s Catholic academic societies: The American Catholic Philosophical Association, the American Catholic Historical Association, and so forth. During this long developmental period, still another reality became painfully apparent. There was no general plan for, nor any coordination in, the development of American Catholic higher education. Colleges proliferated at a rapid rate, very often duplicating each other and sometimes competing with each other. It is thus possible today to find as many as five Catholic colleges in the same city (e.g., Boston, New York, Chicago)— all of them struggling, few of them cooperating to any significant degree with one another.

Hence to the reality of a Catholic intellectual ghetto was added that of vast financial problems. And rarely if ever during these years of development did anyone conceive of the Catholic college as the place where an intellectual elite would be trained; it was considered necessary only that their graduates have some advanced knowledge of Catholic theology and philosophy, and a general education at least no worse than that to be had in secular colleges. As for the members of faculties, it was rarely required that they be outstanding scholars or even have aspirations in that direction. The important thing was that they be good teachers and examples of spiritual and moral rectitude.

Not surprisingly, as the Catholic college system grew by leaps and bounds, one could here and there detect a certain ambivalence among American Catholics toward them. On the one hand, there were those, perhaps the majority, who took the greatest possible pride in their existence. If they were not turning out conspicuously great men, that was not the only thing that counted. They were turning out men (and later women) who could hold their heads up with modest pride, if not in the higher echelons of American life, at least at those secondary levels of society which are no less important. They were fine, patriotic Catholics. What more could one want? But there were those who did want more. By the 1920s there were those who began to wonder why there were so few Catholic scientists, scholars, and civic leaders. Was it actually necessary that, regardless of the standard of measurement one employed, Catholics should fare so poorly? But no sooner were these questions raised than an excuse was ready at hand. The fault—it was said—did not lie with Catholics themselves, nor did it lie in the theory or practice of Catholic higher education. Instead, it lay in the obvious fact that Catholics had been an immigrant minority. They had started out under the poorest kind of circumstances and it was a miracle that they had colleges at all. Sociology, in short—along with the saga of immigrant history— came to the rescue. More, of course, could be done to improve the colleges, but that would take time, patience, and a more favorable social situation.

Such was the pattern of Catholic self-criticism up through the middle of the last decade. At that point, in 1955 to be exact, the influential Catholic historian, Monsignor John Tracy Ellis of the Catholic University of America, published a paper in the Jesuit quarterly *Thought*. It was called, simply enough, "American Catholics and the Intellectual Life." In his article, Monsignor Ellis updated the statistics on the absence of Catholic intellectuals in America. As his predecessors on this subject had done, he paid tribute to the self-sacrifice of American Catholics in creating a massively large system of Catholic colleges; and he pointed out the solid historical reasons why there were so few Catholic intellectuals and scholars. That done, however, he then departed from the usual script. Despite the traditional excuses, he said, "The chief blame, I firmly believe, lies with Catholics themselves. It lies in their frequently self-imposed ghetto mentality which prevents them from mingling as they should with their non-Catholic colleagues, and in their lack of industry. . . . It lies in their failure to have measured up to their responsibilities to the incomparable tradition of Catholic learning of which they are the direct heirs. . . ."

With Monsignor Ellis' article the floodgates were opened. Within the space of a few years, articles by the score and a number of important books appeared from all sides. No longer was very much heard of the immigrant struggle, and the self-congratulations which Catholic educators had earlier showered upon themselves gave way to an intensive self-analysis. Now the analysis turned on Catholic shortcomings. There were too many colleges, too few good ones. There was too little emphasis on intellectual excellence, too much on manual theology and philosophy. There was too much emulation of some of the less inspiring aspects of American secular higher education—an emphasis on business courses and athletics, for instance; there was too little on the standards of excellence maintained by the great American universities—experimental programs for the specially gifted, adequate time and funds for faculty research and publication, freedom from puerile restrictions and censorships for undergraduates, to mention only a few things.

These were some of the broad criticisms—and yet some of the ones more amenable to reform measures. But there were criticisms which bit much deeper. Thomas O'Dea in his *American Catholic Dilemma* spoke articulately for many when he said that a genuine intellectual life among American Catholics was hindered by formalism, authoritarianism, clericalism, moralism, and defensiveness. One could perhaps improve libraries, reduce teaching loads, select better students. But how could one bring about a total change in temperament, a totally new way of approaching the intellectual life? Obviously something more than money was needed. What?

That is the question which American Catholic educators have been asking themselves ever since Monsignor Ellis abruptly brought to an end decades of blindness to the actual quality of Catholic intellectual life. Since that time things have not been the same. The public debate and agitation have subsided, but the hard work is now going on. Precisely because this work has just started, it is impossible to pass judgment on American Catholic higher education. On the whole the Catholic colleges remain inferior. They are inferior to the great American non-Catholic colleges and they are inferior when measured by any but the most modest goals which the Catholic colleges themselves would like to achieve. At the same time, the reaction to the recent self-criticism of Catholic educators indicates a capacity for renewal and exploration; no institutions which have the capacity to pass an unfavorable judgment upon themselves can be prejudged. A whole host of new programs and projects are afoot and we can only wait and see what happens.

Nonetheless, it is possible to ask whether a genuine reformation of American Catholic higher education is *probable*. It is certainly conceivable, but is it *likely?* To answer this question it is necessary to ask one that is still more basic. Will American Catholic educators be able to learn profitably, first, from the historical experience of American Catholic higher education, and, secondly, from the experience of the non-Catholic academic world?

Let us look at the first part of that question. It appears to me that the American Catholic experience shows that it is impossible to have a first-rate university when it is cut off from the mainstream of American intellectual life. The Catholic university can only be a meaningful university if it is a full partner in the national, pluralistic, academic community. In the past, the Catholic university was conceived as an alternative to the non-Catholic institution. If the theory was understandable, it still meant that the Catholic academic world became a closed circuit. The result was an ingrown academic life. Catholics neither contributed much to the broader intellectual community nor did they take much from it. Even when Catholic scholars attempted to confront those problems which exercised the non-Catholic intellectual community, they usually did so too late to make any useful contribution to the discussion. Thus even today when Catholics, with energy and sincerity, try to take their place, they often suffer the handicap of a great time lag. They cannot fully keep up because they have too little contact with non-Catholic intellectuals and currents of thought to enable them to be in at the start of trends, movements and changes. They can only act and respond after the fact.

No less important, it appears that the traditional American Catholic university approach to theology and philosophy has had some disastrous consequences on Catholic intellectual life. This approach can be characterized by describing the main assumption which has motivated the teaching of these subjects. The assumption is that the Catholic Church has, in the course of its long history, developed a definitive and detailed body of thought and doctrine which should be passed on intact to the student. Thus in both philosophy and theology, students have been provided with textbooks which attempt to codify and systematize the "truths" of Catholic thought. Unfortunately, this venture had had three harmful effects. First, it has meant that the students themselves generally find their theology and philosophy courses the most boring and least stimulating; and, even worse, the courses which appear to have the least relevance to their lives. Second, since these courses are too often taught in an atmosphere precluding the exercise of a student's critical intelligence, they tend to stultify the development of a critical intelligence in all areas of his academic work. Third, it does violence both to the nature of theology and to that of philosophy.

Fortunately, many Catholic educators recognize these deficiencies—I am saying nothing new here. Yet I am not sure that they have even begun to arrive at a solution. One result, for instance, of the critique of college textbooks in philosophy and theology has been a number of attempts to develop better ones. Perhaps this is a worthy goal; but it still seems to presuppose that the best thing for students is a textbook—a systematic secondary source. One might suppose that the experience of the past would have shown that a careful reading of primary sources would be much more profitable and stimulating for students. But that has rarely been tried; hence, the tendency is to refine old methods instead of attempting to begin afresh.

Let us look now at the second part of my question. Will Catholic educators be able to learn profitably from the experience of the non-Catholic academic world? The main fruits of this experience seem to me to be the following: that a competition among conflicting points of view is productive of a vital intellectual ferment; that students do far better work and gain more from their education when they are stimulated by their teachers to be critical and independent in their judgments; that a sharp distinction between faculty research and teaching is untenable; that institutional traditions and practices should be re-examined constantly and immediately rejected when they no longer serve their original purposes. Other conclusions could be mentioned, but these will suffice.

They all point in one direction. The more open a university the more likely it is to be creative, alive and productive. If pluralism is, in the first instance, a practical necessity in the secular university, it turns out as well to be an asset in the intellectual order. In theory, one might expect that the most creative university milieu would be one in which all faculty members shared the same ultimate goals and worked, in their diverse ways, to contribute to its achievement. This has been at least one important assumption, I would suppose, held by those committed to the denominational university. In practice, however, it seems to work out in just the opposite way: the greater the babel of tongues, the more dynamic the university. In American Catholic education today it is generally assumed that a new, more comprehensive vision of goals and ends is needed. Yet, oddly enough, those universities which seem to have the most impact on the American intellectual climate are those which are very scant on institutional vision but very strong in urging each individual to create his own vision—or get along without one at all, if he so chooses. The secular university, paradoxically enough, seems successful precisely because it cares so little for ultimate values and so much about creating here and now the concrete conditions conducive to personal freedom.

There is, of course, some basis for a Catholic rejoinder about the purported "success" of the secular university. Even if one grants that they establish the intellectual trends of the nation, produce the most creative scholars, and turn out the future leaders of the body politic, what do they contribute to the spiritual welfare of mankind? What do they have to say about God? These are pertinent questions—but only if their intent is not to evade the problem of quality in Catholic education. Unfortunately, however, many American Catholic educators have an ambivalent attitude toward the most eminent American secular universities; they both envy them for their achievements and scorn them for their secularity. Yet it may well be the case that it is their secularity which helps to account for their achievements. Or, to put the matter more precisely, it may well be the case that the "openness" of the non-Catholic university accounts for their achievements; and that it is not necessarily the case that to be "open" is tantamount to being "secular" in the pejorative sense of the term.

Here we immediately encounter the central dilemma of contemporary American Catholic higher education. Can there be such a thing as an "open" Catholic university? The non-Catholic universities have afforded a practical demonstration of the value of the "open" university. They provide a neutral ground on which men of all persuasions can meet, talk, and, normally, wrestle with one another over their personal versions of the truth. They are committed as a group to nothing ultimate—except, of course, to the "truth" (which is resolutely left undefined). But for the Catholic university, it appears, such neutrality would be impossible. By its very nature, as it is understood today, the Catholic university is committed to Christian values. It is not, and cannot be, neutral about the Word of God revealed in Revelation or about the Church's authoritative teachings on the meaning of that Revelation. On the contrary, the Catholic university has, at its very basis, the duty of attempting to incarnate this commitment in all its work: in its teaching role, in its scholarly role, and in its civic role.

There is, it seems indisputable, something magnificent and eminently logical about this conception of the Catholic university. But it also appears, inexorably, to rule out the kind of creative neutrality which accounts in great part for the achievements of the secular university. Moreover, when one has ruled out the possibility of a radical critique of one's fundamental commitments, does this not close the door on that spirit of untrammeled inquiry which marks the secular university and which is one of its major strong points? These are very difficult questions to answer. To be sure, it is quite possible to reply, and very correctly, that a commitment to Christian truth is not bondage but the essential condition of genuine freedom. But this is a theological reply; it points the way, but does not in itself provide a blueprint for the Catholic university. In practice, on occasion, the commitment is present, yet the sense of freedom which should accompany it is not. Why should there be this discrepancy?

The American Catholic experience provides some reasons. In the first place, lacking solid scholarly respectability, the Catholic university often appears to seek social respectability. It has neither the self-confidence nor the solidity of great age to chart its own course regardless of public opinion. Hence the initial impulse is always toward the safe approach to any challenge. Unsure of its own position in American life, it seeks to avoid controversy— to avoid those radical analyses of men and institutions, mores and fads, which must always be the work of intellectuals. More than that, the Catholic university seems to strive for impeccable respectability within the Catholic community as well. Until very recently at least, American Catholicism has been a conservative and timid Catholicism. This has meant that university administrators have been subject to Catholic pressures toward conformity and passivity. They have had to worry about upsetting the bishops, the parents of their students, their lay and clerical trustees, and financial supporters. They had neither the will nor the fortitude to chart their own course as they saw fit. For the administrators in particular, this has meant that care and caution have become the course of wisdom. Seek the truth—but do not alarm the bishop, do not unsettle the students, and do not become known as hotbeds of radicalism.

Secondly, the relationship between clergy and laity in the Catholic university has been an ambiguous one. In the non-Catholic university, there would be no special difficulty about faculty criticisms of university policy—these would be expected and tolerated, subject only to the ordinary dangers of criticizing men in high places. But in the Catholic university, the faculty today is predominantly lay and the administrators (excepting a few rare cases) priests. In such circumstances, the faculty critic is in a doubly difficult position: a criticism of university policy is tantamount to lay insubordination toward the clergy. Even when that is not at all the intent of the lay faculty, and even when the administration itself tries not to see it in that light—even, that is, under the most charitable circumstances—it is difficult to keep the scent of anti-clericalism out of the air. Often enough, unfortunately, it is in fact distinctly present. The net result is often a sense of great strain on the part of both clergy and laity. Not only, it seems, do clerical administrators feel themselves forced to protect their educational authority, but they also feel constrained to protect their priestly dignity and status. Whether intended or not, the clerical administration of the university often appears to the lay teacher to be a closed and inviolate province. And the lay teacher frequently reacts with bitterness, ceaseless private gossiping, and silent rage at his exclusion from those high decisions which affect the life of the university. It is needless to elaborate why this kind of atmosphere does not encourage the full flowering of Christian freedom; and it is as debilitating to the clergy as to the laity.

Thirdly, the Catholic university in America has been infected with one of the great diseases of post-tridentine Catholicism: the belief that the Church is best served by a public image of perfect internal Catholic unity and harmony. The Church, of course, is one and unity is of its essence. Yet this does not mean that Catholics cannot or should not differ with one another, or that all problems have been solved perfectly once and for all. Yet this is the myth that the Catholic university is prone to perpetuate: by its dislike of public controversy among its faculty members, by its presentation of a bland and pasteurized theology to its students, by its fear of the outspoken professor or the wayward, skeptical student.

Perhaps these three causes of a lack of full freedom in the American Catholic university are endemic to every Catholic university, regardless of national peculiarities. I cannot make any judgment on this point. But I am certain that in America they account for part of the failure of the Catholic university to achieve its own goals, and its failure to be taken with full seriousness by the non-Catholic community.

To say these things does not, however, answer the question whether there can be such a thing as an "open" Catholic university. So far the experience of the American Catholic university in this respect is not encouraging. But the fact that this question is now beginning to be asked provides some new grounds for optimism. In the end it will only be asked directly and forcefully when the Catholic university begins to gain poise, independence, and self-confidence. If one takes the Church universal as one's model, then it seems apparent that the most difficult dilemmas of our age are being confronted. By this I do not mean that this confrontation is necessarily widespread. Instead, I mean that one can find scattered men and scattered groups dealing boldly with particular issues, and taken together this work adds up to an impressive attempt to confront the contemporary world.

The first task of the American Catholic university will be to create an atmosphere open to all that is taking place in the Church—the taking seriously of even the most danger-laden minority positions to be found among concerned Catholics. If even that much can be accomplished, the American Catholic university

will be well on its way toward creating a readiness to respond with
energy and creativity to those immense developments taking place
outside the Church. To be "open" is to be Catholic. It is only
through the failures of Catholics—their fears, their uncertainties,
their quest for respectability—that there now appears to be an
inherent contradiction in the idea of an "open" Catholic university.

II

So far I have dealt in large generalities. I will now try to offer
some specific suggestions toward the creation of Catholic colleges
and universities as "open" in practice as they are now open in the
grand realm of pious abstractions. Let me say, though, that while
one can make specific suggestions about specific problems and
points of friction, it would be a mistake to think that a university
can achieve vitality in a piecemeal fashion. Genuine reform can
only mean total reform. To take a bold step in one direction while
refusing to move in a like direction on related issues is almost to
guarantee that the bold step will itself be nullified. There cannot,
in short, be partial openness, or selective openness, or regulated
openness. If a university is not willing to go the whole way, it
should not claim it is serious about reform.

1. *Administration.* A good place to start is with the administration of the university. By and large, most Catholic universities
are now owned and operated by religious orders; the few exceptions are Pontifical Universities and diocesan colleges. In principle,
there need be no objection to the control of universities by religious orders. From the viewpoint of finances, the gaining of
accreditation, and the formation of a curriculum, religious orders
undoubtedly have manpower available to do the necessary work.
It actually takes comparatively few trained people to administer
even a very large university. If efficiency were the only problem,
there would then be comparatively few difficulties. But a university
requires far more than that to stay alive. It requires vision, flexibility, bold and dynamic leaders. At once, a problem arises. Is
there any guarantee that the religious order controlling a given

university will always and necessarily have such leaders available? Of course there can be no such guarantee. By limiting the upper echelons of university administration exclusively to members of the order, it is almost certain that a very narrow range of personnel choices will be available. If a university is lucky, it will find brilliant men; if it is not lucky, it won't. The main point, however, is that the requirement itself is bound to limit the choice. A university controlled by an order will not be able to choose the best men available; it will have to choose the best men available among members of the order—and, by the sheer law of average alone, it is improbable that the best member of the order will often turn out to be the best possible university leader.

There are other drawbacks as well. Most religious orders have venerable traditions, traditions which are slow to change. Rarely are these traditions—with all their attendant regulations and practices—designed specifically to turn out university presidents, deans, and departmental chairmen. In fact, most orders have taken on the running of universities because of one or another historical accident. Normally, they have other commitments above and beyond the furtherance of higher education. They may have done a splendid service toward higher education throughout the course of history, but this is still not their sole concern. And as it too often happens, unfortunately, their broader concerns can interfere with the proper operation of a university. A manpower shortage in the missions can mean the transfer of an outstanding educator or scholar. The need to train novices for an order often heavily dictates the shaping of curriculums in many smaller Catholic colleges. Personal contacts between priests and students, nuns and students, are frequently curtailed by the spiritual and disciplinary norms of an order. Broad university policies are frequently subject to review and approval by religious superiors who may have little or no personal knowledge of a particular university.

I think there is only one reasonable solution to all of these difficulties. Gradually, but surely, the religious orders should work toward relinquishing control of colleges and universities. This

could be done in many ways, but most easily by gradually form-
ing a board of trustees comprised of persons not members of
the order, and by then turning control over to them. Should it
seem fitting, they might request that the new board of trustees
always have at least one member of the order—a member with
one vote only, but whose presence would remain a symbol of the
origins and history of the university. Should an order recoil from
this radical a move—and many surely would—then the order
should at least determine that henceforth it will pick its administrators from the best people available, including both laymen and
secular priests within the scope of potential candidates. Member-
ship in the order would, then, cease to be a basic requirement for
the actual administration of the university.

2. *Clergy and laity.* Much of what was said about the administration of a university can be applied in this context also. There
is no guarantee that priests can operate a Catholic university
better than the laity. The only reasonable norm should, once
again, be the selection of the best people available. Since in many
universities there are now more laymen on the faculty than priests,
the odds are that the "best people available" will be laymen—
and all the more so as time goes on. To put it bluntly, no consideration of clerical status and dignity should enter into the
choice of personnel. Training, competence, skill, and imagination
should be the sole criteria for university advancement, whether
to the administrative or upper professorial ranks.

This principle can also be extended to the teaching of theology and philosophy. Both are disciplines requiring technical skills
and advanced training. Priests have no monopoly on theological
wisdom; their main advantage is that, until recently, they could
get the kind of graduate training denied to the laity. This is now
changing with the development of graduate lay programs. The
advancement of the laity into theology should, within a couple
of decades, mean a full supply of lay theologians. I can only repeat
my main theme: training and competence should be the only
applicable norms for the appointment of theology instructors and
theology professors. More sharply, no priest should be allowed to

teach theology unless his competence is up to the level maintained by his lay theological colleagues.

3. *The teaching of theology and philosophy.* The question of who should teach theology and philosophy is only part of a broader question: how should theology and philosophy be taught? This is a delicate matter. My own impulse is to answer that they should be taught with no consideration whatsoever for canons of orthodoxy. I believe this is a defensible position if understood in a certain way. Clearly, "orthodoxy"—a notoriously vague word—has a bearing on Catholic theology. There are some positions a person cannot hold, some lines of thought one cannot follow, some propositions one cannot enunciate, and still claim fidelity to the Roman Catholic Church. It is the duty of the magisterium, responding to and articulating the faith of the entire Church, to determine in what this fidelity consists. A theology or philosophy professor who does not know the teachings of the magisterium, or does not inform his students about them, would be an irresponsible professor of Catholic thought. He would be equally irresponsible if he failed to present these teachings fairly and accurately, giving proper attention to their significance for Catholic believers.

But is it also essential that he require his students to personally assent to these teachings as a requirement for satisfactory grades? This does not follow at all. Whether a student accepts the teachings or rejects them is a matter solely between the student and his conscience. As important as his assent may be for his personal spiritual welfare, it is a matter of no *academic* significance whatsoever. The only consideration from an academic viewpoint should be the extent and quality of a student's mastery of the material presented to him in his course. In no other courses are grades and academic honors determined by the faculty's judgment of a student's character; such a judgment should not enter into the consideration of a theology or philosophy faculty.

I will go a step further. If it can be determined that a theology professor is well trained, a fair and balanced teacher, then it is equally irrelevant whether he himself personally accepts the teachings of the magisterium. Unless someone is prepared to demonstrate that it is necessarily impossible for a non-believer to teach Catholic theology with understanding and insight, I don't see how one could, in principle, reject such a professor out of hand. This would mean, then, that there could be a place on Catholic theological faculties for Protestants, Jews, agnostics, atheists, and apostate Catholics. Unlike the situation with the non-believing student, however, I would not argue that it is totally irrelevant what the professor personally believes. Academically, it could well be irrelevant, but in terms of the broad purposes and directions of the Catholic university, the commitments of a professor take on a different complexion. The issue can only be dealt with in its totality by considering what the purpose and spirit of the Catholic university should be.

4. *The idea of a Catholic University.* As an initial, minimal statement, let it be said that no university should call itself Catholic unless it intends its work to be a manifestation, deepening, and implementation of the faith of the Church. This should be understood very broadly, taking in the Church's faith in human dignity, in the inviolability of the human conscience, in the power of reason and reflection, in the value of the temporal world and man's temporal concerns, and of course the Church's faith in the saving Redemption of Jesus Christ, its faith in its own mission to proclaim the Gospel, and its faith that God has sent the Holy Spirit to dwell in the Church. A college cannot call itself Catholic in the fullest sense if it conceives of its purpose as indoctrination or community image-building or protecting students from "the world." More precisely, a college cannot call itself Catholic if this is in fact what it does, even if it stoutly denies that such is its intention.

What is required to implement a full Catholicity? Broadly speaking, it seems to me proper for a Catholic college to require, at the time of hiring, that its theology and philosophy professors be professed Roman Catholics. This requirement could be a good deal more flexible—perhaps a general ideal only—in other departments. But note that I said "broadly speaking" and "at the time of hiring." The point of the first phrase is that there should be ample flexibility to hire non-Catholics should the situation seem to demand it. This would probably arise should a college desire to provide courses in Protestant, Jewish, and Oriental religious thought, to pick only one obvious case. Courses like this could of course be taught by Catholic specialists, but there would be some obvious advantages in hearing about these religious traditions from authentic adherents. So too it could well happen that a theology department might desperately need, say, a Scripture professor and be unable to find a qualified Catholic. The department would then be only sensible if it tried to find a competent Protestant. In philosophy it could easily happen that a certain important field could not be covered by the Catholics available. Again it would be only sensible to find a non-Catholic rather than neglect the field altogether. Or it might happen that a distinguished non-Catholic was available to teach in an area already covered. I think a university would be very foolish if it passed up a chance to get the man solely because he was not a Catholic. In other words, let a Catholic commitment be a general norm for theology and philosophy instructors, but one admitting of many exceptions.

The second phrase I used, "at the time of hiring," is no less important. If at that initial point a person is a professed Roman Catholic, then (all other professional considerations being equal) he should be allowed to remain on the faculty regardless of what happens to that commitment later on. Should he cease to be a Catholic, or come to hold heretical positions, and this does not impair his teaching, then the change should not be held against him. One can grant that such a change could well pose some subtle problems. Yet I see no other way to insure the fullest protection of a professor's freedom to follow his scholarship, reflection, and conscience wherever they may lead him. A Catholic college which penalized a professor for his honest convictions by the threat of a job loss, would be giving the worst kind of scandal to its students and its faculty members. It would be exercising coercion of conscience, either before or after the fact, and such coercion would make a mockery of the word freedom. Undoubtedly many outside the college would be scandalized by the presence of such a person on a "Catholic" faculty. But a college should have the courage to endure the protests and shocked sensibilities. At all times, whatever the outside pressure, it should remain faithful to its own commitment to freedom. In that way, the faculty will come to know that the university stands behind their work, their freedom of research and publication and speech and, most of all, that it is willing to let them be themselves.

With these words I have already implicitly sketched what I take to be the "idea of a Catholic university." It is a university with a predominantly Catholic faculty, joined together as a cooperative scholarly and teaching community, each member of which is given the fullest possible scope to pursue and express the fullness of Catholic and human truth as he sees it.

5. *Student spiritual and intellectual life*. One essential aim of a Catholic university should be to introduce its students to the thought and spirituality of the Church. This aim should go hand in hand with their introduction to the riches of all human thought, whatever its source. At the same time, this introduction must take place in an atmosphere of freedom. Concretely, this means there can be no orthodoxy requirements imposed upon students. The disciplinary requirements of the university (and there will have to be some) should be based only on the physical and academic well-being of the students. This means that there can be no imposed spiritual demands (required chapel or Mass attendance, required retreats, and the like). Everything, absolutely everything, bearing on a student's personal spiritual life should be left voluntary. A university should do everything in its power to attract students to a more fervent spiritual life, a deepening of their faith and commitment; but it should demand nothing from them in this respect.

On a less significant level, the student should be free to come and go as he chooses, be free of direct supervision, be free of rigid class attendance rules, and be free—for better or worse—to direct his own life. The university should make clear to students, parents, and the outside community that it does not intend to stand *"in loco parentis."* It should be willing to offer every kind of help and guidance, but it should make clear that it is going to treat students as adults and expect of them conduct appropriate to adults. Since this kind of freedom almost insures that some students will abuse their freedom, that there will be "incidents" from time to time, the university will have to gird its loins against the outcries of the local community, parents, Church dignitaries, the alumni and trustees. It will just have to make clear to them (and many will never understand) that no considerations of public respectability or acceptance will deter it from giving the students full personal freedom.

An important element of this freedom will be student control of student activities. They should be free to form whatever organizations and clubs they want; free to publish newspapers, magazines and periodicals without censorship; free to invite to the campus any speakers they choose. Needless to say, they will from time to time do foolish things, say foolish things, and generally act like foolish children. This the university will have to bear, grating its teeth if necessary. The only limits to this freedom should be those required by good academic order. Student extra-curricular activities should not be allowed to interfere with the normal teaching process. Beyond that, they should be left to their own resources.

Behind all of my conclusions on these various aspects of student life stands one central conviction: students must learn the meaning of freedom by exercising freedom, by the hard but inescapable school of trial and error. There is just no other way. They will make mistakes, but they need to make mistakes. But on occasion, they will triumph against the "wisdom," the nervousness, the prudence, the timidity of the adult, respectable world. They need the chance for this kind of triumph. They need to discover that the general standards upheld by "respectable" adults, the "tried and true" ways of supposedly civilized, orderly life, are sometimes worth nothing at all by any ultimate test. Only by discovering this on their own will they be able, as adults living in the world, to develop the strength and the perception to live lives of imagination, vision, and integrity. Their time in the university may be one of the only times in their life when they will live in an atmosphere of genuine freedom and openness. It will be up to the faculty and the administration to create this kind of atmosphere, to sustain the students in their errors and their triumphs, and to do everything humanly possible to place before their eyes everything that man has thought and done.

Would all of these reforms insure an "open" Catholic university or college? Unfortunately, no human system has ever been devised which can always and under every circumstance guarantee freedom and openness. My own suggestions are open to many lines of criticism, many quibbles, many exceptions—the problem is just too complex for a perfect solution. But I believe that a solution lies in the general directions I have outlined. If the Catholic colleges and universities can find it within themselves to leap into this dangerous world of freedom, they would serve not only the Church, but they would serve the entire human quest for truth. The only road to truth is the road of freedom. All the other road signs lie.

PART IV

Freedom, Order, and Integrity

CHAPTER TWELVE

Liberal Catholicism in America

ET ME MAKE A FLAT ASSERTION, ONE WHICH I HOPE WILL NOT seem unduly chauvinistic. The numerical, financial, and social development of Catholicism in the United States within the past two centuries has been one of the most remarkable features of modern Roman Catholic history. Note that I say "the numerical, financial, and social development" and not, for instance, the "spiritual, intellectual, and theological development." These latter have been impressive in their own way, but hardly such that one could speak of them as remarkable. On the contrary, one of the striking features of American Catholicism is that its interior development has not kept pace with its exterior growth. In these respects, it is characteristically American. Very much like the American Protestant churches and the American people its genius has been in building, expanding, adding, moving horizontally rather than vertically.

The result is a rich, huge, materially dynamic and institutionally sound Church. If at one time the American Church was something of a pariah in American life, the election of John F. Kennedy in 1960 signaled the end of that era. Not only is the Church rich, then, it is now also respectable. Yet as often happens with rich and respectable men, much of its thinking has been derivative, unimaginative, and prone to remain attached to tried and proven ways. With only occasional exceptions, it is a Church which has not caused much trouble in the community. Excluding a few select areas—most notably, sexual morality—the American Catholic hierarchy and the great mass of people whom they serve are indistinguishable from other people. They have been good, solid citizens who can be counted on to lend support to the prevailing social, political, and economic consensus. One can go a step further. American Catholics are so well assimilated into American life that some are now beginning to be found, for the first time, at the fringes; they are beginning to contribute a small share to radical liberal movements at odds with the national consensus. That share, however, is just enough to emphasize the fact that the overwhelming majority of American Catholics stand squarely in the middle of the road.

Taken together, these dominant traits of American Catholicism can be both a source of hope and of distress. To take the distress first, it often strikes many Catholics—particularly those who could be called political and theological progressives—as perfectly appalling that such a rich and now secure Church should provide such little national and international leadership. Its theologians of international stature can be counted on the fingers of one hand. Its scholars fare little better, either nationally or internationally. Its visionary political leaders, its prophetic social thinkers, its creative economic planners are no less scarce. This litany of complaints could be continued almost indefinitely, but that would be unwise. Boredom with the complaints set in long ago and it would be infinitely tedious to repeat them here (which is hardly to say they are no longer valid).

It would be more useful, and certainly fresher, to indicate the solid grounds for hope. The standard explanation for American Catholic deficiencies has for decades been based on its immigrant origins: the long-time hostility of Protestant Americans; its initial poverty; the early dearth of a theological and intellectual culture; the need to create buildings and facilities first, and so on. On the whole, this is a valid enough explanation, deficient only in speculating whether the type of theology and spirituality available during the nineteenth and early twentieth centuries was of a nature to breed a temptation toward external power, ecclesiastical materialism, and a defensive, individualistic piety. However that may be, the very material strength and security of American Catholicism should now provide a solid base from which to begin a development in other, richer directions. For that is the other side of the immigrant-origin theory: once Catholics established themselves, they could begin exploring those dimensions of life, thought, and society which had to be slighted by earlier generations. That day has arrived, and the theory can now be tested. Is it likely that a significant breakthrough will take place?

Before trying to answer that question directly, it would be useful to take a brief look at some of the main patterns which have marked the history of American Catholicism. They have set the stage for whatever the future will bring and, in addition, provide some useful clues about the direction it could take.

Prior to the American Revolution, the Catholic was in a notably awkward position. There were only a handful of priests, hardly any churches, and nothing at all in the way of an organized ecclesiastical structure. In addition, Catholics suffered many legal penalties and this, together with their dearth of numbers, tended to keep them quiet and unobtrusive. The one thing which helped lighten their burdens was the fact that they spoke the same language as their Protestant neighbors, came from much the same kind of English background and shared the values common to propertied classes with an interest in economic prosperity and stability. Their only shortcoming was their religion, and for this they had to pay a price.

But it was not an unbearable price after the middle of the

eighteenth century, and by the time of the Revolution Catholics were reasonably well accepted. The Revolution solidified their position and what their loyalty during the war could not by itself accomplish the Constitution could. The guarantee in the first two articles of the First Amendment to the Constitution of a separation of Church and State meant that religious freedom was as much their right as that of any other American.

Historians have often referred to the period just after the Revolution and prior to the onslaught of massive waves of immigrants beginning in the 1830s as a time in which the Church could "catch its breath." The expression is apt. Beginning in 1789, the Church was able to accelerate its material development in many important ways. In that year the first bishop, John Carroll, was appointed, the first Catholic college was founded, a seminary was established, and a start was made toward organizing the clergy. The fact that the Church continued for some decades to be primarily English in its ethnic roots was of no small social help, though the presence of a number of emigré French priests created some internal difficulties. By and large, the laity were helpful to the clergy and to the newly formed and rapidly expanding hierarchy. The only major source of friction came in the numerous trustee controversies, most of which turned on the question of the right of laymen to control the spiritual destinies of parishes along with their legal control of parish finances. It is not hard to guess how those struggles came out, and it was only a matter of time until the bishops managed to put an end to trusteeism and have all church property placed in their name.

The trustee disputes, however, were to leave an enduring wariness among the clergy and hierarchy toward laymen—particularly laymen who, they felt, were apt to let the spirit of American democracy go to their heads and demand something of the same freedom within the Church which they experienced in society. Herein lies one important element of what has been an enduring tension in American Catholicism. From the outset of the Republic, American Catholics have been noteworthy for their unbounded patriotism. No protestations of fidelity to the flag, no rhetorical pledges of civic devotion, have ever seemed excessive. No doubt part of this spirit can be explained by the need of Catholics to defend themselves against those who believed that Catholicism and democracy are intrinsically incompatible. But that is only part of the explanation, and just as important a part would have to be credited to the genuine enthusiasm felt by all Americans for the system of liberty guaranteed by the Constitution. Yet it was the kind of enthusiasm, and still continues as such, which was bound to place the quite different system of Catholic obedience and discipline in a harsh light. No wonder, as in the instance of trusteeism, that conflicts between bishops and priests, bishops and laymen, and priests and laymen would inevitably break out now and then. Nor is it any less surprising that Church authorities would from time to time have second thoughts about the spirit of American freedom when they felt its force among their flocks. As an antidote they sought, and got, a tightly organized structure.

Rebellion, or even vocal dissatisfaction, requires self-confidence, an articulated sense of values different from that of the ecclesiastical establishment, and a reasonably high degree of education and purpose. After the suppression of trusteeism in the early decades of the nineteenth century, there was little chance for these characteristics to develop among the laity or the lower clergy. Once the immigrants from Ireland, and then Germany, began to arrive in large numbers, the situation of Catholicism changed in many drastic ways. The early social and intellectual leadership of the Anglo-American group shifted to immigrant hands. The clergy and hierarchy, by dint of a superior (though hardly good) education, became the natural leaders of the immigrants, taking up the same role of dominance they usually had in the old country. If these immigrants were Irish, as they were most apt to be, they were also docile and fearful, gladly willing to be protected and led by their spiritual betters, especially when this promised them some significant help in adjusting to the strange ways of a new and not always friendly land. It was, on the face of it, a good exchange, but it meant that independence, initiative, and imagination had little chance of developing. The main job at hand, for no one seriously proposed any other, was the development of the material, political, and social strength of the Church and of the Catholic community.

If the success of this growth was in many ways praiseworthy, and all the more so in the light of frequent outbursts of violent anti-Catholicism, there were drawbacks as well. One of the most notable, especially in terms of later consequences, was the absence of a developed sense of social justice among Catholics. This was painfully the case with the Abolition movement preceding the Civil War. As seems to happen so often with rising minority groups, the persecutions and injustices suffered by those on a still lower rung of the social ladder are a matter of only faint interest. So it was with Catholics in the face of Negro slavery. Not only were they generally opposed to the movement to free the slaves, but they were able to supply, for good measure, some theological arguments of their own to support the retention of slavery. The principal argument against the Abolitionists was that the sudden freeing of the slaves could produce widespread social disturbances. While it would be desirable in the long run for the slaves to have freedom, the best way to bring this about was by gentle, patient, moral persuasion. This line of argument, with its emphasis on gradualism and social stability, is a familiar one, resorted to time and again by Catholics in the face of pressing demands of justice.

There were also other influences at work in shaping the Catholic attitude toward slavery. One of these was the still-high concentration of Catholics below the Mason-Dixon line, with an orientation and set of attitudes primarily Southern. Another was the pronounced inclination of Catholics to vote with the Democratic Party, a party which, while it was receptive to the Catholic immigrant, was also dominated by Southern interests. Still another influence was Catholic hostility to almost everything "Yankee," including, very prominently, hostility toward the kind of moral crusading which was a mark of New England and Northern Protestantism. This last point has a special importance, for it was in "Yankee" circles that the genesis of American social and political liberalism occurred. By decisively cutting themselves off from this group—the antipathy, it must be said, was mutual—Catholics were for decades doomed to be outsiders to American liberal thought. Only when there were questions of the rights of the working class were ideological detentes possible, but then only sporadically and more as parallel streams of social concern than as a genuine alliance. The failure of Catholics for many decades to enlist in the cause of systematic social justice, a failure abetted by a persistent suspicion of government reform efforts, meant that Catholic social liberalism had to develop its own private rationale and justification.

As it happened, the publication of Pope Leo XIII's encyclical *Rerum Novarum* in 1891 provided just the rationale that was long needed, and it came at a timely moment. During the last few decades of the nineteenth century, a small liberal voice began to be heard in the Church, centering especially around a number of articulate and thoughtful laymen. A lay Congress in Baltimore in 1889 marked the full flowering of this group, and the publication of *Rerum Novarum* two years later meant that their social liberalism now had firm theological backing. They made the most of this support, and a major theme of a second lay congress, held in Chicago in 1893 in conjunction with the Columbian Exposition, was the need for social justice, peace between labor and capital, the evils of unchecked capitalism, and the value of Catholic cooperation with non-Catholics in matters concerning the common good. While no significant reconciliation between Catholics and secular liberals took place, Catholic liberals now had the kind of authoritative support they needed to begin their own development.

Unfortunately, the burst of vitality which marked the end of the nineteenth century was doomed to flag for a time with the arrival of the twentieth century. The condemnation by Leo XIII in 1889 of "Americanism" and the Modernist crisis shortly afterwards called a temporary halt to the emergence of liberalism. For at least two decades thereafter, Catholic intellectual and cultural life was overshadowed by a nervous conservatism, which hampered both the attempts to better adapt Catholicism to

American democratic ideals and to create a strong theological culture within the Church. One of the few bright spots during these dismal decades was the work of a handful of social thinkers, most notably Father John A. Ryan at the Catholic University of America. They continued to explore some of the openings provided by *Rerum Novarum* and, of equal importance, trained and inspired a number of priests toward increasingly bold thinking and action on the political and economic front. This was in turn passed on to a growing body of socially sensitive laymen.

A major breakthrough, however, only came in the aftermath of World War I. An important stimulus was a document with the formidable title "Social Reconstruction: A General Review of the Problems and Survey of Remedies," published in 1919 and signed by a committee of bishops. This document, which came to be known as the "Bishops' Program," urged immediate reforms to bring about a living family wage and looked forward to the day when the majority of workers would at least own part of the instruments of production. The ground was thus well laid for further advances and consolidation, at least so far as official sanction was concerned.

The only missing element, the social confidence and milieu necessary for liberal development, was gradually supplied. Catholic service during World War I, the prosperity of the twenties, and the fact of an almost complete cultural assimilation, quickly swept away the fog which lingered on after the Americanist and Modernist upheavals. Though Catholic theology in America was far from being creative, and the earlier emphasis on material development continued, the twenties saw the appearance of a fresh cultural and intellectual life. My own journal, *Commonweal*, began publication in 1924, the first serious Catholic lay publication since *Brownson's Quarterly Review* in the middle of the nineteenth century. Catholic historical and philosophical associations were also formed and there were expressions of concern from many quarters about the failure of Catholics to make any significant contribution to American intellectual life.

But it was not until the thirties that this renascence began to have some bite. As had happened with *Rerum Novarum* forty years earlier, Pius XI's encyclical *On the Reconstruction of the Social Order* in 1931 provided a major prod to American Catholic social thought. The National Catholic Welfare Conference took the lead on the official level in stimulating "Catholic Action" and in bringing before the public issues of political and economic justice. No less important, the thirties saw the founding of the Catholic Worker Movement, led by Dorothy Day and Peter Maurin, and a consequent acceleration of Catholic radicalism. Though the Catholic Worker group was comparatively small in numbers, it served as a rallying point for a new generation of Catholics who saw in the Great Depression solid evidence that *laissez-faire* capitalism was unjust and economically destructive. Only a lingering alienation from secular and Protestant liberalism, as well as pervasive fears of being labeled a "pinko" or "commie," kept the new Catholic liberal from forcing strong bonds with other liberal and radical movements in America. In the years following World War II, however, American Catholic liberalism became a well-established reality, needing only the work of Vatican II to insure its permanent strength.

This brief sketch is necessarily incomplete. It made no mention of the growth of Catholic education, of the rising level of Catholic participation in national politics, of the Catholic political domination of most of the major cities of the Eastern seaboard, of the response to urban life by immigrants from a predominantly rural background. All of these elements would have to enter into a full history of American Catholic liberalism. One could hardly afford to neglect, for instance, the lamentable fact that Catholic political power in Eastern cities was not matched by a corresponding zeal for urban reform; indeed, civic corruption among Catholics seemed almost a way of life in cities like Boston and New York. But that is a story which cannot be gone into here.

Yet enough has been said, I trust, to provide a tentative answer to the question raised earlier: is a significant breakthrough in Catholic thought, especially Catholic liberal thought, now likely? The answer, I believe, has to be yes. More than that, the breakthrough has already taken place and what remains is to see how far it can and will go. The present situation of the Church in America is one of unprecedented vitality, and this vitality is being experienced on a wide variety of fronts.

Easily the most important sign is to be found in the steady and increasingly deep self-criticism which has been a mark of the Church for the past decade or so. Hardly anything has been spared: Catholic education, the hierarchy and clergy, the laity, and on and on.

Though many have complained about the self-criticism, calling for "moratoriums" on "breast-beating" and "masochism," "less negativism" and more "positive thinking," their words have had little effect. Where in earlier days Catholic liberals were given to complaining about a conservative domination of the Catholic press and intellectual life, it is now the conservative who is likely to complain about a "liberal conspiracy." Naturally, complaints of this kind lay a heavy stress on the "few" and "unrepresentative" people who, by a sleight of hand, manage to convince an "uninformed" public that their views represent those of the majority. To a certain extent this is no doubt true. Very few conservative Catholic thinkers have managed to achieve any special distinction or to gain a public following; thus one hears very little about them or from them. At the same time, as Catholic liberal thought has gained a public ascendancy and continued to expand the range of its thought and criticism, signs of a backlash have begun to appear. This can be seen in a number of statements issued by individual bishops within the past couple of years deploring "arrogant" laymen, a dangerous spirit of disrespect for authority, and the tendency to extend self-criticism into the very heart of theology and doctrine itself. Other signs can be found in many diocesan papers, where both editorial writers and letters-to-the-editor display considerable uneasiness about the advance of liberal thought; in a small movement like that of the "Traditionalist Society," established to combat a "protestantizing" of the

Church; and in the reluctance of many bishops and priests to do more than minimally observe the spirit of Vatican II.

But it is important to distinguish between a backlash and the broad direction of the Church. As in the Negro civil rights movement, a backlash is itself persuasive evidence of where the major winds are blowing. It can hurt and stall progressive trends, but only rarely does it make a decisive difference to the movement forward. At any rate, there is no evidence yet that the growing conservative episcopal, clerical, and lay worries are about to effect a major reversal of the fortunes of Catholic liberalism. There have been very few successful attempts on the part of conservatives to silence the liberal critics and reformers; actually, comparatively few attempts have been made. The more dramatic instances of stress and strain do not, however, provide the only clues to the future of Catholic liberalism. There are at least three other important trends with a very important bearing on the question.

The first of these is the entrance of the layman into the thickets of theology. Until less than ten years ago, American Catholic theology was exclusively in the hands of the clergy, and then only a handful of priests at that. Moreover, the quality of American theology was third-rate, Roman and legalistic in its spirit, derivative in its speculations, and almost wholly lacking in any special character or genius. The Catholic University of America, which might be a central source of theological creativity, has never been a major university. With the exception of the Jesuit quarterly *Theological Studies,* and the *Catholic Biblical Quarterly* there have been no reputable theological journals. Only John Courtney Murray, S.J., has achieved any kind of international standing. Though they might have been expected to do so, the Catholic colleges and universities have produced nothing in the way of distinguished theological scholarship; until very recently they only aped the methods and preoccupations of seminary theology.

The entrance of laymen into theology promises to help change the situation. Within the past decade, graduate programs in theology have been started in a variety of Catholic universities; a number of Catholic colleges have begun hiring laymen to teach theology; in the bloom of ecumenism, a sizeable group of secular universities have invited Catholics to teach in religion and religious studies departments; and the influx of Catholic faculty members has been far exceeded by the number of Catholic students who have undertaken graduate work in theology and religion at secular universities, even Protestant divinity schools. The significance of this trend is likely to be twofold. First of all, it should help broaden the base of theological education and the number affected by it. This will help break the grip of the seminaries and assist in the creation of a theology which is integrated into the mainstream of American higher education. Second, it should help create a body of theologians far more relaxed and far more independent of ecclessiastical bureaucracy and timidity than was possible for priest-theologians under the watchful eye of bishops and religious superiors. Doubtless this will mean from time to time some aberrant, indeed clearly heterodox, lay theologians writing and teaching, but these will probably be only a small minority. What the majority (and even the radical minority) could succeed in doing is not necessarily to produce better theological work than that of priests, but a theology which springs from a different situation in, and perspective on, the world. The greater freedom of the layman, together with his different perspectives, should in turn serve as a healthy stimulus to the work being done by priests.

Quite apart from the professional work done by academic theologians, clerical or lay, there should also be a greater boldness on the part of broadly educated and informed laymen to venture opinions on theological questions. Already a small number of lay publications do not hesitate to comment critically on issues dealing with the inner life and structure of the Church, on theological disputes and the pronouncements of Church authorities. In an earlier generation, even highly educated laymen rarely spoke on such matters, though they would have felt no hesitation in speaking on other issues which went beyond their academic or professional training. The notion, once revered, that a Catholic could not claim responsibility for beliefs and practices imposed upon

him by the Church, that his only duty was docility and trust, finds
fewer and fewer adherents.

A second important trend might best be characterized as a
new willingness of Catholic liberals to take their opinions, grievances, and crusades "into the streets." Prior to the last few years,
very few Catholic intellectuals or social action advocates were
prone to take strong and public stands on their convictions and
positions. They were careful, timid, and given to delicately couched
opinions; rarely would they make known either to the Catholic or
the non-Catholic public how they really felt about various problems within the Church. Much of this has now changed. The
presence of numerous priests, nuns, and laymen in civil rights
demonstrations; the frequent circulation of petitions directed to
one or more members of the hierarchy; public protests of abuses
within the Church; blunt articles in Catholic newspapers and
magazines—all of these things signal a new spirit, one marked by
an absence of timidity in the face of authority and a drive toward
open discussion and argument. Despite a number of episcopal
admonitions, the problem of birth control has been vented from
all viewpoints, with very few reluctant to express their uneasiness
about the teaching of Pius XII. On other fronts, lay groups have
picketed chancery offices, priests have risked censure to take part
in racial protests, and hardly any lay writers now seek an *impri-
matur* for their writings. For those of a more traditional cast of
mind, none of these changes are happy omens. But for those
committed to a deepening of Catholic liberalism, they are minimal
conditions for an effective Christian witness and dialogue.

A third important trend is the significant extent to which
non-Catholic thought, both religious and secular, is drawn upon
in matters theological as well as secular. Closely related to this is
a genuine breaking down of many of the barriers which kept
Protestants and Catholics, and Catholic liberals and secular
liberals, alienated from each other. Ecumenism in America has
become a living force within the Church, if not always on the
popular level, at least very much so in academic and intellectual
circles. This has meant a serious attention by Catholics to

Protestant thought and scholarship. References to Karl Barth, Rudolf Bultmann, and Dietrich Bonhoeffer are almost as common now in American Catholic writing as references to Karl Rahner, Hans Küng, and John Courtney Murray. Since so many Catholics are now studying theology under Protestant auspices, the impact of ecumenism is bound to be even greater in the years to come.

If the alienation which kept Catholic and secular liberals apart for so long is disappearing in a less noticeable fashion, it is, nonetheless, giving way to a new relationship. The civil rights movement and the gradually more active participation of Catholics has been one solvent. Catholic participation in demonstrations against nuclear weapons and the Vietnamese war though involving very few people, has been still another. It is not difficult now to find Catholics openly willing to call themselves socialists, to commend the welfare state, and to express agreement with many aspects of Marxism. The liberal élan of John F. Kennedy, as well as that of some of his Catholic advisers and assistants, did much to suggest to secular liberals that the Catholic could be a potential ally. That the overwhelming majority of Catholics voted for Lyndon B. Johnson in 1964 (over seventy percent) rather than Barry Goldwater was further evidence that the Catholic community has no special predilection for right-wing politics. The hysteria in many Catholic quarters during the McCarthy area of the early fifties was no permanent index of an innate conservatism.

I have dwelled very much on the hopeful side of the picture, but only because, for one who has seen many dark days in years past, the present ferment is exciting beyond description. At the moment, it seems fully vigorous enough to withstand any immediately foreseeable backlash, any letdown in Rome after the Council, or even any failure of the American bishops to extend the frontiers provided by the Council. Yet much is still missing and it is easy to conceive of circumstances which could alter the present direction. The most noticeable soft spot is the American hierarchy. As a group the American bishops are hard workers, full of good will, little given to suppressions, and relatively innocent of the kinds of Machiavellianism which mark some episcopal groups. But like their predecessors they remain primarily administrators, little alive to the newer currents of theological thought or to the currents which move through American intellectual life. Hardly a handful has ever written a serious book or article and their speeches, sermons, and statements give little indication that they regularly read such books or articles. Though it is true that the American bishops quickly became identified with the progressive majority at the Council, it is not easy to resist the belief that they did so more out of conformity with the rest of the bishops— because that was the way the wind was blowing—than out of personally achieved thought and conviction. On the whole, they have gone no further in implementing reforms in America than those minimally required by the conciliar constitutions and statements. One is bound to wonder whether, should the winds from Rome shift in any significant way, the American bishops would quietly and quickly shift without a murmur—that has been their tradition in the past. There is no way of telling, but it is far less certain that the American hierarchy would show a respectful independence than, say, the German or Dutch hierarchy.

What seems most likely is that Catholic liberalism will have to get along without enthusiastic and imaginative support from the hierarchy. But there are many mitigating circumstances. Despite their many qualms, the bishops as a group remain permissive. That is a tremendous asset, as helpful a virtue in bishops as any reformer or experimenter can realistically ask for. It is a virtue far less frequently found in chancery offices. For it is in those offices, rather than in episcopal palaces, that narrowness, bureaucracy, and timidity reach full bloom. The wise priest in America discovers at any early age that he should not ask permission from a chancery functionary to do anything faintly novel unless he absolutely can not avoid it. The same can be said, though less harshly, of diocesan officials, organization supervisors, superintendents of this institution or that. As much as anything, however, they are victims of an ecclesiastical system which is cumbersomely large, forced in the direction of bureaucratic impersonality, and too harassed to have much time for sensitive human relationships. However great the penetration of liberal ideas may be in other quarters of the Church, they have made few inroads into the machinery of administration, fund-raising, and economic planning. For it is not ideas which are threatened here so much as empires; they are proving durable and hardy.

The parochial school system is a special case in point. Despite the publication in 1964 of a widely discussed book by Mary Perkins Ryan, *Are Parochial Schools the Answer?* (which concluded: not necessarily); despite the results of some studies showing that the schools have not achieved results in proportion to the time, money, and single-minded zeal which have gone into them; despite the presence of much dissatisfaction with the way in which the American parish, financially and spiritually, has almost become an appendage of the school—despite all these objections, resistance to discussion, experimentation, and the consideration of other methods of religious education still continues to be the rule in official quarters. (The only point that seems to make any difference is the financial troubles of the schools; they can galvanize bishops and school superintendents to act imaginatively where no other considerations seem to have any influence at all.) There is a faith in the schools, and a zeal for their welfare, which is proof against any statistics, questions, and alternative suggestions. So much is this the case that the Bishops have not hesitated to throw their weight against urgent federal education bills if the funds involved did not also benefit the parochial schools. This intransigency has not been wholly ineffective as a strategy. The American public is more willing now to consider providing some money for aspects of the religious schools than at any time in the past. But it has also meant some forcing of Catholics back into the mold of ghetto isolation and self-centeredness, fighting for their own rights at the expense of the improvement of public education.

Problems like this wax and wane in the Catholic community, but they usually serve to drive a wedge between those Catholics committed to broadening the concerns of the Church beyond matters of immediate self-interest, and those who seem to believe that what benefits Catholics must necessarily benefit the whole nation. Some of the sharpest conflicts between the ecclesiastical establishment and Catholic liberals come when the latter judge the duties of the Church in the light of national needs rather than in terms of institutional Church needs. Many Southern parochial schools, for instance, were very reluctantly and slowly integrated, and the main argument of those responsible for establishing policy was that the schools would suffer financially, that it was not their duty to provide leadership, and that community sentiment would be hostile toward the Church as a result. The legitimacy of arguments like this, which placed the physical survival of the schools and their financial solvency before all other considerations, was violently rejected by Catholic liberals. In turn, the liberals were criticized for their supposed insensitivity to local problems, their willingness to sacrifice long-established institutions for the sake of problematical results, and so on.

What is at stake in an argument like this goes well beyond the practical issues involved. It involves the very broad question of the way in which the American Catholic should relate his religion to the society in which he lives. Let it be granted that, once upon a time, Catholics had little choice but to seek first the consolidation and strengthening of their own social and financial condition. Their weak, struggling position left them few options, and the hostility of Protestants was enough to deprive them of the chance to make constructive contributions to the national good. But this has now changed, and any further excuses in this respect will carry no weight.

The American Catholic liberal is now in a position to do at least three vital things. First, he should feel fully free to enter into working alliances with non-Catholics for social and political reform. If he does so, then the parallel liberal movements which so often existed in the past should now be able to unite, resulting in the enrichment of both. Second, the stage is well set for a renewed attempt to work out the theological dimensions of the American experience. This task was aborted by the condemnation of "Americanism," but has since taken on a new life because of the work of

John Courtney Murray. Yet he has only scratched the surface, and much remains to be done. This task would inevitably carry with it the need for creating an American theological idiom, which could draw on native resources and cease being so dependent upon European leadership. Third, the Catholic liberal can take full advantage of the renewal taking place in the whole Church. Now is the time to press long-delayed questions. Now is the time to try new things. Now is the time to bring everything out into the open. It might well happen that a serious reaction could set in after the Council—such seems to be the common rhythm of movements in the Church. With this possibility in mind, however remote at the moment, the liberal could at least insure that, whatever his fate, posterity would have some fruitful questions, suggestions, and ideas to work with. The advice of the tradition to reformers is finesse, patience, and diplomacy. The lesson of Vatican II is that bluntness, boldness, and impatience can be even more productive.

Yet to suggest the possibilities and opportunities open to Catholic liberalism is by no means to say that they will be realized. On the whole, there is bound to be some progress in the years to come. Even those who at one time were doubtful about many things dear to the hearts of liberals have now swung over. There are no serious doubts any longer about the necessity for a more vigorous theology, or better Catholic universities, or the need for an atmosphere of freedom in the Church. Nor are there many doubts about the need for an effective social witness, some structural reforms at the diocesan and parish level, better seminary education, and a greater reliance on the layman. Even with some degree of reaction against those who press for rapid reforms, who continue to find new aspects of Catholic life to criticize, the momentum is likely to continue in a forward direction.

Nonetheless, there are the ingredients of a serious crisis lurking just below the surface. These ingredients are not easy to describe, for they are as yet inchoate, but they have certain things in common. Perhaps the most important is that they each involve a very radical questioning of some central points of Christian and

Catholic belief. One does not, for instance, have to search very hard to find some who wonder about the contemporary validity of the "supernatural"; they have taken to heart the enterprise of demythologizing Scripture and Christian doctrine. Nor does one have to look far to find some who wonder whether the idea of the Church as a hierarchical society has had its day; or whether the Church can, without falling into idolatry, claim any binding authority; or whether the doctrine of papal infallibility was simply a very bad mistake on the part of the Church.

Speculations of this kind do not appear in print, for reasons both obvious and subtle. The obvious reasons are the certainty of a major explosion should anyone dare express such questions openly and the practical impossibility of finding Catholic journals which would tolerate their publication. But the subtle reasons are probably more important: a recognition on the part of those with such problems that they are, even by the most liberal standards, skirting the edge of serious heresy. That recognition, taken alone, would probably be tolerable, the price that has to be paid for a deeper penetration of the Gospel. But there is an even deeper perception that outright heresy is too costly to the Church, that the price paid for progress of that kind is too high—the price of disunity, of the hardening of factions, of bitter and harmful acrimony. Of equal importance, those who raise such questions do so in a speculative way, not in the manner of determined revisionists fully equipped with alternative theologies, but rather because a full attempt at renewal seems to entail a radical willingness to investigate afresh the traditional fundamentals of Christian belief. The result is, to say the least, a very complicated stance, both theologically and psychologically. With equal vigor it affirms the necessity of a common creed and the necessity of a free investigation of the validity of that creed.

Let it be said, at this point, that I am only offering an interpretation of the direction of some Catholic liberals; no one has quite put the matter this way. Most liberals would in fact repudiate the suggestion that they have any difficulties with basic doctrines. But I want to assert they do, and that a close observer of the printed word and a careful listener in the small hours of the morning can find many clues to support this judgment. No doubt many of the bishops sense what is happening. Though they are easily refuted when they try to argue that some given book or line of criticism *proves* the bad faith of those they attack, their instinct for danger is reasonably accurate. The authority of the magisterium *is* being challenged, though not always or even most of the time in the ways in which the bishops think it is. Quite correctly, however, they have discerned that the effect on some Catholics of the Church's effort at reform has been to throw almost everything into question.

Hence, if one is to ask about the future of Catholic liberalism, one has to ask what the consequences of this drive for a total reexamination of Christianity and the Church are likely to be. My own guess is that some serious struggles are likely to take place, quietly at first but eventually on the public stage. They will not be struggles in the old style, between those who want the Church to stand perfectly still and those who want it to make some vigorous efforts toward renewal. On the contrary, the struggles are likely to take place within the liberal camp, between those who feel that the Church can and should change—as long as nothing fundamental is called into doubt; and those who feel that partial renewal is self-defeating—that only the most courageous and total questioning will suffice to insure a meaningful change. Since it will not be easy to reconcile these two positions, open conflict seems inevitable.

The severity of the conflict will depend upon two things, the possibility of expressing daring ideas and developing radical lines of thought in print and on the public platform, and whether those who want to do so continue to abide by the traditional rules of the game. There is no special reason to suppose that the first condition will not gradually come about. If it is not yet possible in America for every conceivable issue to be discussed fully in print, it is possible at least to touch on everything—provided this be done in a circumspect way, with a plentiful number of scriptural and theological citations and in a tone which is that of respectful speculation and mild wonderment. As for the second condition, the question here is whether the radical speculators and questioners will continue to observe the *de facto* etiquette which normally sets rough norms or standards for the pressing of new issues in the Church. At present this etiquette demands—if I interpret it correctly, for it is of course more implicit than explicit—that one proceed cautiously, in a tentative way, expressing frequent words of humility, docility to authority, and a willingness to let one's work be judged by those more competent than oneself. Moreover, the etiquette demands that one keep one's radical speculations from the public eye, submitting them first to other professionals and ecclesiastical authority, and only if they have met approval there taking them into the public domain. As part of this constellation, the etiquette requires that, if rebuffed by the professionals or by authority, one retreat into silence, mulling over one's missteps and, perhaps, attempting to recast one's thoughts in a more acceptable fashion.

Such, I take it, has been the pattern adhered to by most Anglo-Saxon theologians for many decades now. Yet there is a real possibility that this pattern will break down. A fair number of Catholic writers have discovered that some Protestant journals are open to articles by Catholics on Catholicism which might not, because of the line they take, be accepted by Catholic journals. Again, since most lay writers no longer seek imprimaturs, the possibility of totally circumventing the censorship system is now a full reality. Finally, the new public interest in matters Catholic, stimulated by the Council, means that Catholic writers can place their articles in secular papers and journals; hence, there will be even fewer restraints on the Catholic who wants to voice opinions which would be unacceptable to the Catholic community as a whole or to the episcopacy. I am glad that these possibilities are now available (and I have made use of them myself). At the same time I think it necessary to recognize that developments of this kind—making possible a totally unfettered criticism and speculation—are likely to make the bishops increasingly nervous (for there will be no easy means of control available to them); are

likely to encourage at least some to develop their thought quite
independent of and indifferent to ecclesiastical authority and
judgment; and are likely to stimulate, and lend credence to, those
who feel that the new spirit of freedom in the Church has opened
a Pandora's box. The possibilities for instability, serious crises, and
open struggles in this kind of situation should be obvious. That
they will come I do not doubt. How they are handled will, more
than anything else, determine the future of Catholic liberalism in
the immediate years to come.

CHAPTER THIRTEEN

The Quest for Honesty

WHILE IT WOULD PROBABLY SMACK OF IRREVERENCE, THERE ARE times when I wish it were possible to feed into an advanced computer some knotty problems of religion. At the moment there are two I would give it. The first, a general question: How long does it now take for an idea which originates in the secular world to make its appearance in religious writing? The second is more specific: How long does it take before problems which agitate Protestant minds begin to agitate Catholic minds?

The questions are not as idly speculative as they may sound. For surely a competent computer, with the aid of a few historians, social observers, and literary men feeding it raw data, could have predicted some years ago that Catholics would eventually take up the cry for "honesty" in the Church. The idea of "honesty" has been, after all, a critical one in the post-war secular

169

mind: writers are extolled for their honesty, their sincerity; political scientists are forever "candidly" speaking their mind about political myths; psychotherapists have been telling us how much we lie to ourselves; someone or other is always condemning us for lacking the courage to tear away at the falsehoods in our society. When one hears Catholics finally talking this kind of language, whether it be for "honest" reporting in the Church, for "honest" talk about Catholics and family planning, for "honest" admissions that the Church needs reform—one can only say: "aha, it's come."

The odd thing is that however quickly Catholics pick these things out of the air, Protestants have often been there first. Again, a computer could probably have predicted that just as Catholics would begin tentatively talking of honesty, many Protestants would be in the midst of a full-scale debate on the same point. The most prominent sign of this is that prodigious Protestant best-seller, *Honest to God* (Westminster Press, 1964), written by the Anglican Bishop of Woolwich, England, John A. T. Robinson. Less noticed, but in much the same vein, is *Objections to Christian Belief* (Lippincott, 1964), a set of lectures by four Anglican theologians at Cambridge. The point of both books is to take a hard look at "traditional" Christianity, subjecting both creed and morality to unflinching examination. In particular, the various theologians aim to set forth their doubts and worries, not in order to destroy Christianity but rather to achieve some sort of harmony between what the modern world takes for granted about reality and what, by contrast, they think Christian theology says about it. There is also an implicit consensus among the authors that Christians today do not, in fact, give as much credence to traditional thought as they themselves think; and that this is the source of considerable dishonesty.

The Catholic quest for honesty, if I interpret the clues correctly, has now reached a point at which many are discovering that what bothers them is not this or that specific problem, but more: that it is so hard to speak openly in the Church. Difficulties seem concealed altogether or buried beneath carefully laid layers of sanctimonious optimism. John Cogley put it well recently when he wrote that he would like to see the "layman feel free to express his convictions, doubts, and dissents without fear of 'violating orthodoxy' or seeming to be brash. . . ." Yet it would be a mistake to identify too closely the Protestant and Catholic quest.

No Catholics, so far as I know, are suggesting, as does Bishop Robinson, that a lack of honesty in the Church is keeping them from expressing radical doubts on the "mythological" world-view of the Scripture writers, on the very idea of "supernaturalism," or on relevance of "religion" to Christianity. Yet it is precisely this kind of "honesty" which Bishop Robinson wants. If not, there will be, he believes, "an increasing alienation, both within the ranks of the church and outside it, between those whose recipe is the mixture as before (however revitalized) and those who feel compelled to be honest *wherever* it may lead them." "We are being called," he thinks, ". . . to far more than a restating of traditional orthodoxy in modern terms. Indeed, if our defense of the Faith is limited to this, we shall find in all likelihood that we have lost out to all but a tiny religious remnant." What, practically, does this mean? "We have to be prepared for *everything* to go into the melting . . . even our most cherished religious catagories and moral absolutes. And the first thing we must be ready to let go is our image of God himself."

Honesty, however, can cover a multitude of sins and virtues. Understood one way, it can simply mean the opposite of hypocrisy, which is a concealing of one's true beliefs beneath a veneer of conformity. Understood another way, it can mean a radical willingness to take nothing as too sacred for searching examination, a willingness to pay whatever price is required to get to the bottom of things. Bishop Robinson seems to use the word in both senses. On the one hand, he thinks many Christians do not in fact believe in certain elements of traditional Christianity nearly so strongly as they pretend to. On the other, he thinks that Christians lack the courage to face their own irrelevance and so are prevented from taking the steps necessary to confront modern man.

All of this may sound vaguely familiar to Catholics, as if an amplification from another room of the debates centering around the Council. The similarity is there, but the differences are pronounced. One difference is Bishop Robinson's belief that even the best kind of revitalization of old Christian doctrines will not do any longer. Another is that he has been influenced by those elements of recent Protestant thought which have remained outside the mainstream of Protestant-Catholic ecumenism. From Rudolf Bultmann he has taken his criticism of a continuing Christian dependence on the three-layered "mythological" imagery of the Bible; from Paul Tillich his rejection of traditional theism; from Dietrich Bonhoeffer his critique of what Bonhoeffer called the "religious premise," i.e., that there exists a "supernatural" sphere over against the "secular."

There is still another difference, one best expressed perhaps in A. R. Vidler's introduction to *Objections to Christian Belief*. There Dr. Vidler asserts that "the objections are likely to be perceived and felt even more keenly by people who, maybe for years, have been living with one foot in Christian belief and the other resolutely planted in the radical unbelief of the contemporary world, so that they are, as it were, torn between the two." Clearly Bishop Robinson is such a man, as are the contributors to *Objections*. Yet I daresay there are few Catholics who would care to describe their tensions in this way (however suitable such a description might be). For the most part, Catholics approach unbelief as something which exists *outside* of the Church and *outside* of the believer. The possibility that unbelief may exist within the Church, even among the solid "faithful," seems rarely to cross the minds of most Catholic writers. The merit of Bishop Robinson's book and the authors of *Objections* is that they take this coexistence of belief and unbelief within the heart of the believer with full seriousness.

It is worth noting a certain oddity here. While it could be expected that many conservative Anglicans would react violently against the ideas expressed by Bishop Robinson and his Protestant mentors, the sharpest attacks have come from some non-Christian philosophers. The English philosopher Alasdair MacIntyre, for instance, said of *Honest to God* in an *Encounter* review: "This book testifies to the existence of a whole group of theologies which have retained a theistic vocabulary but acquired an atheistic substance." Of Paul Tillich's work Sidney Hook has commented that "I am not fully persuaded that Tillich's ambiguities can get the idol-worshippers out of the temple; there is some evidence that his ideas provide the rationalizations for those to remain who otherwise would have left." The same attitude is prominent in Walter Kaufmann's *Faith of a Heretic*. For these men, the new "honesty" is in fact the worst kind of dishonesty.

One of the few points I can see with any clarity here is that "honesty" is a classic example of a weasel-word, the use of which depends almost entirely upon one's starting point. In the case of Bishop Robinson, much of what he rejects in "traditional" Christianity is in fact not traditional at all. Instead, it is what the popular mind thinks Christianity is, quite a different matter. The unfortunate thing is that the Bishop himself only half-realizes this; thus many straw men are destroyed in the name of honesty. Again and again he distorts traditional theology. How honest a procedure is that?

In any case, I am reasonably certain that Catholics cannot long remain out of the fray. Bishop Robinson's book is a harbinger of more to come. Sooner or later our own quest for honesty will probably take some to that "radical questioning" which Bishop Robinson calls for. What is surprising is that the Hooks, the MacIntyres, and the Kaufmanns have managed so far to overlook the Catholic efforts at renewal initiated by Pope John. Surely they could find something to say about the twists and turns of the conciliar debates, especially about the "new insights," "deeper understanding," and "expanded horizons" of the progressive majority. For it is a fairly good rule-of-thumb that whatever appears suspect to the conservative theologian will be just as suspect in the eyes of some non-believers. Each will accuse the innovator of selling out, however different the grounds for their objections may be.

That this is so makes everyone's task that much the harder. When everyone begins shouting for honesty, and all condemn self-deception, one can only expect confusion.

So far, thankfully, we haven't reached that point in the Church. The idea of honesty still remains a fresh one. But can we keep it that way? Much will depend upon our ability to be both thorough and creative in our honesty. The way to be thorough is, in the very first instance, to realize how honesty itself can be a form of self-deceit. (The most common example of this in our day is the homage paid to self-confessed egoists: they are at least credited for being "sincere"; the rest of us are hypocrites.) Creativity is even more important. Unless we ruthlessly explore our own motives, biases, and hidden impulses, searching in every nook and cranny of our mind and emotions, we are likely to fool ourselves as much as ever.

The best example of creative honesty I have run across recently is a passage in Father Karl Rahner's translated collection of essays, *Nature and Grace* (Sheed & Ward, 1964). After singling out Modernism as one form of "hidden heresy" he goes on to point to another: "[But] much more frequent (although difficult to pin down) is an attitude of mistrust and resentment against the Church's magisterium, a widespread feeling of being suspiciously and narrowly controlled by it in research and teaching, the feeling that 'one can't say what one thinks' (but one is nevertheless justified in thinking it in 'good' conscience). Doesn't one come across the feeling that one can say more (at least among friends) than one can write? Or the attitude that one should be glad that this and that has been said by Protestant theologians outside the Church, and one has to go to them to read it because one could not say it without risk oneself? . . . Isn't there here something like an esoteric teaching which is spread only by word of mouth? Isn't there unformulated heresy which avoids clear exposition in print and works by omissions and one-sided perspectives . . . ?"

That, I say, is honesty; and it hurts. Nor is the pain appreciably lessened when Father Rahner goes on to say that a rigid conservatism can also be a form of heresy: "This freezing of the form in which the truth of the Gospel is expressed is in fact a dangerous symptom of indifference . . . to the truth." One way or another, I fear, Father Rahner's insights on heresy will leave most of us "honest" folks feeling like the emperor when he discovered he was naked.

But it won't do to escape from our nakedness by half-hearted attempts at humor. There is something funny here, but the joke may be on us. Is it in fact possible for Catholics to be wholly honest? I, for one, am not certain. I doubt that the Church is now prepared to accept those who would, willy-nilly, undertake the kind of "radical questioning" which Bishop Robinson has urged upon his fellow Anglicans. Even a serious and solemn attempt would run into a barrage of criticism, if not gaining for its author summary excommunication should he refuse to recant. But the incapacity of the Church to stand this kind of "honesty" is not necessarily a mark against it. The Church teaches with authority. This it could hardly do if it was compelled to put its most central truths up for total debate every time someone felt that honesty compelled him to question them. At the same time, of course, it would be well for the Church, so far as is possible (and that may be much further than we think), to be patient toward its interrogators. Before it dismisses them, let it put some charitable questions to them. Let it take their questions seriously. We desperately need such openness. That way both honesty and truth can be served.

Such encounters will, for the time being, probably be rare. Of greater immediate relevance is the question whether the Church can be honest enough to carry through the renewal sought by the Council. The signs are both good and bad. They are good insofar as there is in practice (if not yet in theory) considerably more freedom for the individual Catholic to speak his mind directly on controverted questions. Many are still fearful of doing so, but it is becoming clear that those who do so do not always encounter the criticism and censure their imagination often conjures up before they take their stand. More than one would-be martyr for honesty has found that, instead of the stake, he gets praise, honor, and money.

There are many bad signs, however. Among the worst can be found in some speeches praising the work of the Council. Of course the Council condemned anti-Semitism; the Church has always opposed anti-Semitism. Of course the Church favored religious liberty; it has always been a champion of a free conscience, of a "free Church in a free society." Of course the Council stood for a free press and free speech; only the misinformed could think otherwise. Each of these statements contains a grain of truth and a grain of falsehood, in about equal mixture. But the way statements of this sort have been bandied about, as the whole truth, is sufficient evidence that we still have a way to go to reach even an approximation of honesty.

In fact, however, the situations just mentioned touch only a few of the different occasions in which questions of Catholic honesty could arise. They can arise when there is discrepancy between theory and practice; when there are unvoiced difficulties about living up to a moral teaching of the Church; when some or many people find a particular argument employed by the Church obscure or unconvincing; when doubts exist that a principle is being properly applied; when many believe that a given teaching, tradition, or custom needs reform; when a general feeling arises that a new scientific, historical, or sociological discovery calls for a fresh look at an old, well-established belief; when there is evidence that an ancient Church law has become outmoded; and so on. The possibilities seem almost infinite.

One problem is that different kinds of self-deception (individual or communal) can come into play in different situations, calling, in turn, for different kinds of honesty. Thus the very fact that the Church's teaching on the immorality of contraceptives is a difficult teaching will mean that it will be just that much harder to be honest with oneself about it. The very fact that one might be willing to admit with all candor that it is difficult might, by the very same token, lead one to escapist doubts about the cogency of that position. Is it not likely that someone caught in a desperate conflict of family planning would be the most prone to believe that the Church's teaching *could* change? Or that it *must* be wrong? Or that it is all the fault of the celibate clergy? To go to the other extreme, would not the person who honestly believed the Church's position is irreformable be the one most likely to be dishonest about the kinds of difficulties which can arise (by shaping facts to fit principles)? It is as if, in both cases, sheer honesty about one side of a problem paves the way for dishonesty about another.

If nothing else, then, one should be wary about where one judges honesty to be required, and what kind is needed. It is easy enough to say "everywhere." But it is rarely going to be that easy. It is one thing to be honest about, say, what one thinks the Church teaches. It is still another to be honest about whether one in fact accepts this teaching. And it is something else again to be honest about how one feels about this teaching even while accepting it.

The secular experience with the idea of honesty, to which we should be indebted, ought to be a warning. As Peter Berger has well put it, "There are, after all, far more sincere liars than cynical ones, if only because self-deception is psychologically easier than Machiavellianism." To this I would add that much in Catholicism offers an enticement to sincere self-deception. Since authority counts heavily in the Church, and the Church makes strong claims, there is every inducement to convince oneself that one is convinced. At the same time, since the Church is authoritarian those who attempt to exercise their freedom can easily come to believe that the forces of repression are inexorably weighted against them. It thus often happens that those who do have the courage to speak out are far more liable to dote on the rebuffs they receive than the praise. It is as if they can only confirm their freedom by dwelling on the price they have to pay for it. Of course since the price *is* sometimes high, their emphasis may not be misplaced.

Well, then, where are we? The banner of "honesty" has been raised. It is a good banner, just as long as the staff on which it is raised does not have worm holes. That means we must be honest about our honesty; and honest about our honesty about our honesty. . . .

CHAPTER FOURTEEN

Birth Control and the Theologian

THE ARGUMENT OVER FAMILY LIMITATION IN THE CHURCH TODAY may be likened to a drama, but one so rich in rhetoric and sub-themes that it is increasingly difficult for the audience to follow the plot. They are not to be blamed for their confusion. The play is constantly being rewritten, new scenes are added with increasing rapidity, and no one has yet been able to devise a satisfactory ending. The critics have not been helpful either. Some see only an old-fashioned morality play: faithful Catholics standing firm against the secularist hordes and their Catholic fellow-travellers. Others see it as a courtroom drama: the people vs. the minions of the law. Still others see it as a tragedy (though they are not always clear who the tragic hero is).

Well, of course all these elements are present on the stage, so each of the critics has a point. But I would like to suggest that the development of the play to date has gradually uncovered what
178

may be the real and lasting issue at stake here: how authority in the Church is to be understood, interpreted, and developed. For that is the one issue which seems most to determine the lines spoken by the actors. Whatever he may privately think, the layman is only likely to speak those lines which he believes are assigned him in the Church. Exactly the same thing can be said of the theologian. Now and then, of course, an errant line escapes from someone's lips (more today than ever); and some of the lines have a double-meaning. Even so, the stage curtain of authority hangs over everything: as a source of confidence for some, anxiety for others, and perhaps as a puzzle for most.

A convenient way to grasp the unfolding of this play is to begin with those changes which have marked the past decade or so. Up until about the middle of the fifties there was a remarkable harmony among the ideals of the magisterium, the theologians, and the married laity. The large family was accepted as the norm of a Catholic marriage, even though it was formally recognized that medical, economic, or other "indications" could justify, for "serious reasons," recourse to rhythm or abstinence. But these indications were clearly thought of as exceptions. All of this brought comparatively few objections from the laity, at least those who might be accounted "zealous" Catholics, or "nuclear" Catholics. Indeed, we are sometimes prone to forget today how the ideal of a large family was once seen by many to go hand-in-hand with the liturgical movement, social justice, and contemporary spirituality.

Social realities, which arrived in a variety of forms, soon unbalanced this equilibrium. Catholics finally realized how much the Protestant consensus had changed, so much so that now family limitation (by the most efficient means) is taken to be a Christian duty. Then the population explosion began to be noticed by demographers, and the early efforts to dismiss their work as secularist propaganda made less and less sense. Of more immediate concern to Catholic parents, it turned out that American society is simply not geared for very large families; that fifteen-room Victorian houses are in short supply; that a family of six, eight, or ten children requires an income well above the average; and that such an ideal, even if physically possible, takes little account of the emotional needs of the husband and wife, much less those of their children. A new perception of the importance of education, of the necessity that a wife be something more than a mother, and that a husband be something more than a bread-winner, helped to round out the change of perspective. Here lies one revolution.

No less important was the revolution beginning to gather speed in the Church. Manual scholasticism, with its baggage of apodictic certainties, showed signs of an impending death. Person-alism, existentialism, and the thought of the Church Fathers began to make more sense and to speak a more meaningful lan-guage. The Bible came into its own, not just as a book to be praised in the abstract, but as a living source of concepts, perspec-tives, and spiritual animation. It too speaks a different language, a language which makes the old books of moral theology appear dangerously inadequate, if not altogether misleading. The Second Vatican Council pushed the revolution forward. To an extent which still remains undetermined, it has called into question many episodes in the Church's past. More importantly, it has cast doubt on many traditional ways of thinking about Catholic doctrine. It shattered old certainties. It showed that Catholics could think unthinkable thoughts (even if it has not made clear how far this can go). It brought the beginning of freedom in the Church—free-dom of conscience, not just that old-time Catholic freedom, the freedom of perfect submission to every iota of the law.

All of this amounts to a theological revolution, of which only the barest hint has shown itself in the Council. Yet all the while this revolution was in the making those I will call the "Center Party" moral theologians have remained firmly imbedded in the atmosphere of the past. In America, probably the finest fruit of the work of this party is *Contemporary Moral Theology*, Vol. 2: *Marriage Questions* (Newman, 1964) by Fathers John C. Ford, S.J. and Gerald Kelly, S.J. Their work over many years, of which this and an earlier volume are the outcome, has provided Ameri-can theologians with detailed and probing surveys of the whole spectrum of moral problems, both practical and theoretical. On the whole, they have steered a middle course between the arch-reactionaries and the pioneers (and thus have been attacked from both sides). For that reason, Fathers Ford and Kelly could be said to personify the center, and *Marriage Questions* to epitomize the thrust of its thinking.

The range of problems covered in *Marriage Questions* is broad, the treatment of them marked with precision and sublety, and the criticism of those with whom they disagree eminently charitable and fair. Among other things, they sketch the development of Protestant thought on marriage, detail the problems posed for traditional theology by the emergence of a school of personalist theologians, present their own *via media* between the personalists and the canonists, and argue their own theory of the ends of marriage. Throughout the first half of their book Fathers Ford and Kelly are preoccupied (in a very illuminating way) with the relationship of the "primary" and the "secondary" ends of marriage. In the second half, they deal with more concrete problems: contraception, sterilization, "the pill," periodic continence, and other matters. On the crucial question (at least in the popular mind) whether the Church can or is likely to change its teaching on the immorality of contraceptives they are forthright. "The Church," they write, "is so completely committed to the doctrine that contraception is intrinsically and gravely immoral that no substantial change in this teaching is possible. It is *irrevocable*." Moreover, they think it "very likely" that the Church has taught this doctrine infallibly (a judgment, of course, disputed by other theologians).

When seen in the light of the double revolution noted above, certain characteristics of Fathers Ford and Kelly's methods are at once apparent. One searches in vain for a heavy use of biblical texts (or even a light use). The primary proof-texts which they employ are papal encyclicals and allocutions and the comments and decisions of other organs of the magisterium. Next in importance are the writings of other moral theologians. The philosophical presuppositions and concepts (which loom large) are drawn almost exclusively from traditional scholastic terminology and that of the canon lawyers. There is only the barest hint that Fathers Ford and Kelly have been much swayed by the theological revolution in the Church.

At the same time, it is important to note, they are sensitive to the kinds of difficulties which confront married couples today. That they do not speak the ordinary language of the laity should by no means be held against them. There is much evidence implicit in the book that they understand this language, and, more than that, that they have heard their share (far more than most laymen) of the anguished cries of couples caught in acute moral dilemmas. That they do not speak in the vernacular themselves is beside the point: they were not writing sermons or popular manuals, but instead write as professional theologians for a professional audience.

In many ways, then, *Marriage Questions* is a model book, once care is taken to note the purposes, methods, and presuppositions of the authors.

It is also a book which, like the theological tradition it represents, is years behind the revolution now in progress. Here lies the tension inherent in the book itself, a tension particularly visible in the authors' fear that a substantial change of Catholic teaching on licit methods of family limitation would have disastrous consequences for the Church's claim to teach with authority. It is this sense that the Church's fidelity to its position takes on a symbolic value which goes far beyond the particular doctrines in question. If the Church changes here, then nothing is safe: that is the unveiled fear which Fathers Ford and Kelly (not to mention many others) cannot help but concede. If there is a theological revolution in progress in the Church generally, then this is one of those critical issues which, in the eyes of many, will mark the difference between doctrinal development and chaos. Fathers Ford and Kelly are wary of the former and abhor (rightly) the latter.

Hardly less important as a source of tension is the way they seem to conceive of their tasks as theologians. The best analogy that comes to mind is that of government civil servants. There is, for one thing, little indulgence in personality in their book. Their tone is that of proper functionaries, ever shy of the first person, self-effacing to the point of psychological obliteration, and totally awed in the face of what they take to be authoritative documents or pronouncements.

Now there is of course nothing traditionally wrong in such a stance. Seen in a less harsh light all of these characteristics bespeak genuine humility and wholly dedicated service to the magisterium of the Church. In other respects, however, it is far more difficult to adopt such a perspective. For it is one mark of the civil servant that he tries to cover up, or gloss over the weaknesses in the position laid down by the high command. He puts, in short, the best face on things he can, keeping as far as possible from the public eye the gaps, the inconsistencies, and the uncertainties of the official policy. This he can do by skirting the hard questions put him, or, if he is a loyally creative civil servant, by inventing ingenious *ad hoc* arguments to cover all eventualities. Still another part played is that of devising a new rationale for an established policy when it has become clear that the old arguments in its favor are no longer adequate.

All of these tendencies are present in *Marriage Questions,* but are most prominent when the authors try to show the reasons behind the Church's rejection of contraception. They are, for instance, aware that the traditional natural law arguments no longer persuade many Catholics. To meet this situation, however, they do not wonder whether the position is defective, but instead conclude that better arguments have to be devised, and that it is the task of the theologian to devise them. Yet since they are also aware that the Church has rested its case heavily on the natural law, they have an inherent difficulty on their hands: how can the position be assumed correct if the reasons once taken to demonstrate it are now seen to be inadequate or incomplete? Their answer is not one to shed luster on the theological profession: "When the Church asserts that a truth is of natural law, she does not *ipso facto* become responsible for providing a convincing demonstration of the truth based on arguments derived solely from reason." It is, they say, "the task of the theologians to elaborate these points." As for the embarrassment inherent in a recognition that the natural law arguments do not persuade, their response is to say that this perception shows the "moral necessity of a religious authority for an adequate knowledge of the natural law." As fast as one prop collapses, then, a new one is devised to take its place. And what are the married laity to do while this work of reconstruction goes forward? Hold fast, naturally, since "for Catholic living . . . internal conviction and external conformity is enough; it is not necessary to know why the Church teaches that contraception is intrinsically immoral." (Fair enough, if that is the way things must be: but if the theologians cannot demonstrate the cogency of the doctrine, why are they and the magisterium so certain that it is correct, much less "irreformable"? One is reminded here of the English philosopher who described the demise of an old philosophical doctrine as the result of a "death by a thousand qualifications.")

At this point, let me say I am aware how harsh this way of approaching *Marriage Questions* and the work of Fathers Ford and Kelly sounds. Any portrayal of obviously dedicated, obviously committed, and obviously sincere theologians as akin to loyal civil servants or faithful party workers is bound to appear offensive. It also has the effect of minimizing unduly their valuable insights. For that I am sorry. Yet it is helpful to take such a special vantage point, for it assists in explaining why the birth control question is such an unusually troubling one for the theory of authority in the Church. It has been urged, for instance, that dialogue between the theologians and the laity is essential. Indeed it is, but what good will that dialogue do if at the very outset the theologian conceives his task as that of defending, developing, and rationalizing an "irreformable" doctrine?

How can the layman possibly trust the theologian if he suspects that the latter never speaks personally but always as the representative of higher authority? Who delimits the lines uttered by the theologian: his own Christian reason and his informed conscience or those he supports as an obedient, loyal servant? There is just no way of knowing. This is particularly true of published works by moral theologians since one knows that to win publication, they had to run a gauntlet of censors. It is also true, however, of face to face confrontations with theologians. There is nothing more painful than to watch a theologian think twice before he answers a direct question; to listen to him carefully and haltingly frame a precise answer which will not put him or the Church in an embarrassing position; to see him twitch and squirm while defending publicly a position which he (and everyone else) knows to be a weak one, or while devising a jerry-built "answer" to a pointed objection. To bring the pain to a fine point, one need only ask of the theologian: What do *you* think? There is little in his role as docile servant which prepares him to confront, much less bare in public, his personal beliefs. For him, they do not count. He is prone to camouflage his private opinions, his attitudes, his way of thinking. In extreme cases, he tries to act as if he does not even exist, or as if his mind is perfectly interchangeable with that of the magisterium. I conform; therefore I am. (Unfair? Yes, but not very.)

I would not want to suggest that such a self-image is incompatible with the creation of genuine theological advances. On the contrary, the numerous Center Party theologians have been responsible for much of the development of doctrine which has marked recent decades: the shift away from the large family norm, the taking seriously of the "secondary" ends of marriage, and the rejection of a purely legalistic approach to family limitation. But it is a self-image incompatible with some essential requirements in the present situation. It is, first of all, vital that the theologian understand not just where his predecessors went wrong, but why. Was it not, for example, a partially false conception of authority which led so many theologians for so many centuries never to wholly reject a tradition which saw any use of sex apart from procreation as dangerous if not sinful? It is just not enough to pass off the rejection of this position as the unfolding of "new insights" or a normal doctrinal development. For centuries a serious mistake was made, one which misled many people. Why?

If the theologian sees himself only as a docile servant of an established doctrine, how can he avoid making the kinds of mistakes his predecessors have often made? He must, secondly, therefore, explore afresh his relationship to the magisterium, asking himself and the magisterium whether his role has been so conceived as to endanger the possibility of unbiased scholarship.

Third, it must be possible for the individual theologian to take, in public, a position counter to that of established teaching if his Catholic conscience and his scholarship so dictate. Otherwise, the layman will never have full confidence in the integrity of the theologian. So, too, the magisterium must allow this liberty to the theologian. Otherwise, it could never have confidence that he was not simply fawning on authority or that a purported theological consensus was the real one. Finally, the whole atmosphere supporting the enterprise of moral theology must encourage the theologian to be candid with himself, candid with his colleagues, candid with non-theologians, and candid with the magisterium.

The birth control question is, above all, a test case for the Church's understanding of itself and especially of its understanding of the development of doctrine. That means it is a test case for the contemporary renewal of the Church. Its importance lies in the direct confrontation of the theological methods and inclinations of another generation with those now emerging. The reason, for instance, why the natural law arguments against contraception are so unpersuasive today does not stem from some suddenly undiscovered fallacy in one step of the argument. Nor does it stem only from a rejection of the premises of the argument. Significant changes rarely take place in this way (though detailed critiques of old arguments normally accompany such changes and are necessary to help them along). They come about, rather, because of a radical shift of perspective, the development of a new group consciousness, the shaping of new conceptual and linguistic tools, and the impact of history and social circumstances. All of these forces are present within the Church today and present within that world of ours in which the Church exists. They are more than just "present": they are operating with a positive fury.

If there is a tragedy latent in this drama, then it lies in the desperation of good people trying to use old tools to cope with new material. It lies also in the desperation of married couples trying to relate old certainties to new uncertainties, holding on by their fingertips to a sandstone ledge they had been assured was made of granite. In each case, the natural inclination is to panic. That is a sensible response, but not the only one possible. A better one would be for the Church, in its teaching authority and in its members, to immerse itself in the present. No theologian today can be expected to be understood if he continues to argue that the primacy of the species takes precedence over the personal good of individuals. He will not be understood if he argues that biological values take precedence over personalist values. He will not be understood if he says that one must accept a doctrine or a law on the basis of authority alone. The problem is not that these things are necessarily wrong. They are incomprehensible, flying in the face of everything contemporary man has learned about himself, about his conscience, about nature, and about value. They have been taught him by the Church as much as by the world. If the concept of a "living magisterium" has any meaning at all, then it must at least mean this: one way to remain faithful to the past is to affirm the present. That is the demand which our life here today has directed to the Church's exercise of its authority. That is the cutting edge of renewal.

CHAPTER FIFTEEN

Is God Dead? .

I THINK ONE CAN TAKE IT FOR GRANTED THAT ANY RADICALLY NEW theological movement is going to be offensive. This is doubly true of what William Hamilton has called the "death of God theologies" in Protestant thought. Not only do they mark a sharp break with most of contemporary and traditional theology, but they also embrace as their starting point what appears to be a denial of the existence of God. The English philosopher Ninian Smart expresses a common enough Christian scorn: "A colleague of mine recently said to me: 'My wife is an atheist, but she wants to be an Anglican as well. Is there anything she can read?' 'My dear fellow,' I replied, 'we've got plenty of books showing how the trick can be done.'"

The word "trick" sounds just right here. What else can be said of a theology which: (a) appears to take seriously the linguistically

188

nonsensical phrase "God is dead"; (b) shares with the atheist a distrust of anything outside of man; and then (c) has the effrontery to assert that it may be possible to give this outlook a solidly biblical basis? One is likely to feel at this point much like Kai Nielsen felt after trying to make some sense of Paul Tillich: "Tillich doesn't put new wine into old bottles, he puts in grape soda and then labels it *Chateau Latour*." But even grape soda is not without its tang and many people have been able to drink it. And what has in the past looked like a mere trick often turned out to be something else again. Ultimately, any "death-of-God" talk means practically nothing, but as a handy expression it has its uses. All it needs is a stiff dose of its own remedy; it needs to be demythologized.

Actually, that is not hard to do. Only one of the members of the new school, William Hamilton, really finds the phrase helpful, and then not for long. Its utility lies, as he put it in a *Christian Century* article (Oct. 6, 1965), in suggesting a "real loss, something irretrievable"; that is the value of using the metaphor of death. By contrast, other phrases, such as an "absence of God" (Heidegger), or the "eclipse of God" (Buber), or a "hidden God" lack sufficient decisiveness. They "still live quite comfortably within the classical tradition of the dialectic between the presence and absence of God." Yet it is soon clear that Hamilton does not at all see himself as a traditional atheist. He affirms the legitimacy of hope and finds it sensible to speak of "waiting for God." His question is: what is God's real role—if we can find Him? The one role Hamilton believes to be entirely ruled out is that of God as a "need fulfiller and problem solver" (*The Christian Scholar*, Spring, 1965). Those things man can do for himself.

Well and good, but how can one call oneself a Christian, holding a position like that? Hamilton is candidly vague. All he can say is that "Jesus is the one to whom I repair, the one before whom I stand . . . there is something there, in his words, his life, his way with others, his death, that I do not find elsewhere. I am drawn, and I have given my allegiance." One could, I suppose, dismiss these words as so much verbal fog; but if commitment to Christ is at the center of the Christian life, Hamilton cannot justly be cast into outer darkness.

Paul Van Buren poses more difficult puzzles. Unlike Hamilton, Van Buren is very clear about his secular starting point and methodology. His standards are those of contemporary linguistic analysis. The task he sets for himself in *The Secular Meaning of the Gospel* is to interpret the Gospel in an empirical way. Why that way? Because that is the way men think today, and it is just as legitimate to attempt a translation of the Gospel into empirical terms as it was for earlier Christians to attempt a translation into Aristotelian or Platonic or Kantian or Hegelian terms. "How," he asks, "can a Christian who is himself a secular man understand the Gospel in a secular way?" The question is a shrewd one, and for Van Buren the answer is that we have to look to the language of Scripture and Christology, attempting to grasp its secular, rather than transcendent meaning. This means that "we must begin where we can, with the realm of the world, open in principle to human investigation, and that means, Christologically speaking, with the true humanity of Jesus of Nazareth." An important offshoot of his dependence on linguistic analysis is that Van Buren sees at once that the expression "God is dead" is meaningless: there is no conceivable way of verifying the supposed fact of God's death. "No," he counters, "the trouble is that the word 'God' is dead." (*Communio Viatorum,* Summer, 1963). It is not easy to argue with him here.

Van Buren's questions, though, are more interesting than his answers. Because he spells out his secular translation of the Gospel in some detail—intercessory prayer, for instance, comes down to reflecting on problems from a Christian perspective and then taking appropriate action—there seems far less room for the possibility of a transcendent God than with Hamilton. His most glaring weakness, however, and the most revealing, is his dependence upon two of the least impressive of the English analysts, R. M. Hare and R. B. Braithwaite. From Hare he takes the notion of "bliks," a word meant to stand for a person's fundamental attitudes, his basic presuppositions, about the world. For Hare, religious assertions are not to be understood as assertions capable of verification or falsification, but as expressive only of ultimate attitudes and orientations. Hence, it is inappropriate to ask whether religious assertions are true or false. Braithwaite's position, fully expressed in *An Empiricist's View of Religious Belief*, is that religious assertions are essentially used as moral assertions: they do not state facts, or tell us something about the world, but, instead, guide our conduct.

There is something to be said for each of these positions, but they both suffer the fatal deficiency of trying to find a single, central use of religious language. If the work of the analysts has clarified anything, it is that there are many very different uses. Hare, Braithwaite, and Van Buren see clearly that the positivists were wrong in judging religious language by the standards of the empirical sciences; but none of them sees that it is equally mistaken to search for archetypal uses of religious utterances.

It may seem something of a digression to concentrate on the way Van Buren employs the philosophers who attract him. Yet I think not. The test of any recourse to secular insights is how they work in their application. A fatal error of the nervous theologian is to rule out certain approaches at the very outset—that is why the very idea of a "secular interpretation of the Gospel" has been dismissed in so many quarters as preposterous. The history of theology, however, is a history of mixed marriages; the families groan but the marriage often turns out beautifully. Van Buren's failure does not lie in taking the line he does, or working from a secular perspective, but in failing to show that it will work successfully. He is quite right in reminding us that "Christians were once called atheists by a misunderstanding, but religious, culture." Yet he does not show that his secular interpretation of the Gospel can achieve his own stated aim: "an interpretation which may claim for a secular Christianity the full tradition of the faith." The Christianity he gives us comes down to a certain perspective on the world and an ethical system. That is not "the full tradition of the faith." His project, though, is worth continuing.

I have concentrated on Hamilton and Van Buren because I find them the most interesting and comprehensive. A fuller description of the movement would have to take account of the work of Thomas J. Altizer and Gabriel Vahanian. I must confess that I find Altizer almost impenetrable, in great part because of his love for dialectical tensions, paradoxes, and mystical flights. A student of Mircea Eliade at the University of Chicago, and now at Emory University, Altizer expressed his aims clearly in an article in the *Centennial Review* (Spring, 1964), "Theology and the Death of God": "If theology is to transcend itself it must negate itself, for theology can be reborn only through the death of Christendom, which finally means the death of the Christian God, the God who is the transcendence of being . . . . The problem for theology . . . is the recovery of a truly dialectical faith in which the sacred and the profane are not separated and in which authentic existence is possible." Once he begins this "recovery" the clouds start to roll in. The result is a new mysticism and a new immanentism, but to describe it here is beyond my powers. Vahanian is less troublesome. He attacks the "idols of religiosity" and the complacency of the Church, and he believes that God will remain dead until the churches have better mastered their secular tasks and are in a strong position to proclaim Him once again. It is doubtful, in fact, that he should even be called a "death-of-God" theologian.

There are many ways of interpreting the whole movement, but one problem seems central to all of these theologians. They want to know if it is possible for one to be a Christian without an awareness of God or a sense of the transcendent. This question has been asked before many times in the history of Christianity, but almost always in a context of a steady faith in God or that of possessing some rational proofs for the existence of God. What does one do if the faith is absent, the proofs unconvincing, the word "God" seems just a noise or a mark—and yet the Christ of Scripture remains a powerful, mysterious, and unique person, who cannot be contained within the categories of that secularity which seems so triumphant and persuasive? That is the question which

I think the death-of-God theologians are asking. So far, the answers they have proposed strike me as blind alleys. Langdon Gilkey, their most perceptive critic, is correct in saying "The effort to interpret Christian theology without God is a failure." Nonetheless, they have asked a valuable question. No one has given them a convincing answer.

CHAPTER SIXTEEN

The New Freedom

THE FRENCH REVOLUTION, ONE RECALLS, BEGAN IN A MILD ENOUGH way. Dominated by a coalition of priests and lawyers, the Estates-General met in a mood of seriousness though not quite of crisis. As we know, of course, one thing led to another, and within half a decade France was in chaos. Never again would that country or Europe be the same. The Old Regime would not return, however many more momentary victories it might claim.

Nor in these days of Vatican II will the Church's equivalent of the old regime return either. Genuine revolutions, those springing from deep and widespread distress, are rarely turned back. Can anyone still doubt that Vatican II has been a major upheaval, not necessarily in its debates and decrees, but in the forces it has unleashed within the life of the Church? These forces were there of course all the time, but it took a decisive event to bring them to the surface. And like every revolution it has generated its own momentum, so that one shift has led to another, one criticism to many, one reform to the unearthing of a dozen more still needed.

A key to this revolution has been well expressed in an increasingly common phrase: "the new freedom." If *aggiornamento* is the spiritual father of this revolution, the "new freedom" is its first-born child. Not yet certain, at least for many, is whether the child is legitimate. The uncertainty is only natural. The child just doesn't look like the father.

What is the new freedom? That is not an easy question to answer, for everyone is likely to see it in a different light. But it may be helpful to look at it in terms of its style, its motivations, and its contents.

The style of the new freedom is direct and earthy, scornful of euphemisms, ornate verbiage, and discreet circumlocutions. In its politer, theological form, it is biblically direct, but with due respect (i.e., minimal) for older forms of theology. In its rougher journalistic form, the style is no less blunt, but the imagery is more likely to be drawn from democratic political and social life rather than from biblical or theological sources. At times, it is downright irreverent, not so much because of real disrespect, but rather because that is the way writing and speaking is carried on these days.

The motivation for the new freedom is that of Christian liberty issuing into Christian manhood, as much liberty as needed to establish personal integrity, as much liberty as can be had without jeopardizing the Church as a community of love. Rejected are suppressions and purges, censorship, curial intrigues, faceless accusers, nervous "prudence." If any phrases can catch the motivation of the new freedom, possibly it is that of *écraser l'infâme* together with that of the "freedom of the sons of God."

The content of the new freedom turns on three or four key concepts, well brought out in the first two chapters of the *Constitution on the Church*. The most important is that the Church is a mystery, a community, a people, not the "perfect society" which the older theological manuals liked to talk about. Understood properly, the Church must of necessity be an open Church, a poor Church, a servant Church, a Church on pilgrimage until the end of time. Seen in all its dimensions, the Church is holy because Christ its founder is holy, but is made up of sinners and is thus also a sinful Church. The Holy Spirit is inevitably seen in a fresh light here. For He it is who at times grants sufficient charism to the laity and the lower clergy, to nuns and brothers, to enable them to make prophetic judgments, to see what authority does not see. Naturally this implies the possibility of rebuking and instructing the hierarchy. Does not the Holy Spirit "blow where He will"? For its part, the hierarchy exists for the sake of service; and the sign of its willingness to serve is its disposition to listen, to humble itself, to limit itself, to take advice. As a constant motif, the new freedom insists upon practice which measures up to the theory. Words must be verified in action; theory must be spelled out in concrete responses and structures.

This brief sketch could hardly manage to catch all the nuances of the new freedom, but it may be sufficient to suggest some of its causes. The Council is surely one cause, but not necessarily the most important. The great contribution of the Council was its demonstration that open debate is good for the Church, that freedom of expression is a liberating power. If the bishops can argue, if they can be uncertain, if they profit from mutual criticism —then can't we all? Yet too much emphasis has been placed on the Council, as if it alone (or together with the spirit of Pope John) explains everything. No less important is the shattering impact of everything meant by the expression "the contemporary world": the impact of a demythologizing science, political and social pluralism, cultural secularity, urbanization—but why continue? All of these things have actually been present for decades, but it took the fact of a complete social assimilation and an awakened sensitivity to secular thought to bring their weight directly to bear on the Catholic consciousness. Almost overnight, all the old apologetic citadels fell and in rushed the world. No one yet knows what to do about it, but at any rate we know that the old distinctions and theological niceties will no longer work. The fate of Pope Pius XII's reputation stands as a good symbol of what is taking place. Rolf Hochhuth's play, "The Deputy," maligned the man personally, but his critique of the papacy's self-conception was brutally revealing. The mark of every revolution is the down-grading of former heroes.

The revolution also has another, decisively important cause: the permissiveness of the bishops and the Holy See. One may well doubt whether the most extreme measures could wholly have stifled the outburst, but it surely could have curtailed it, limiting its scope to the secretive and the agile, the diplomats and liberal scribes. The fact of the matter, however, is that the bishops and the Pope have done little to limit the explosion. To be sure, Pope Paul has assailed those who "seem to have nothing to give Catholic life than bitter, destructive, and systematic criticism," but that was a bland enough complaint, hardly sufficient to deter the critics. (Besides, is anyone likely to admit that his criticism is purely destructive?) And while the scattered remarks of various American bishops indicate some are worried about excesses and affronts to the dignity of the magisterium, it is increasingly difficult to find instances of genuine suppression. The reasons for this permissive-ness are not clear: perhaps fear of public opinion; perhaps, to take the optimistic view, because the bishops and Pope have them-selves been influenced by the upheaval, now realizing that the muscular methods of the past are both outmoded and un-Christian. In any case, it has been a long time now since the last *monitum* appeared.

The "new freedom" has already had many important conse-quences. Problems are now being discussed in a way which would have been utterly unbelievable five years ago; and what is being said in public is innocuous compared with what one hears in private conversations. Escalation is as good a word as any to sum up the course of these discussions. One started by talking about contraception and the "natural law" arguments; now one talks about the possibility of a fallible magisterium. One began by arguing about the religious liberty of non-Catholics; now one affirms the rights of the Catholic conscience. One sought "re-newal"; now one wants reform.

The power of this escalation can vividly be seen in *Objections to Roman Catholicism,* edited by Michael de la Bedoyere (Lippincott, 1965). Here we find many long-accepted complaints, but with a new urgency and force. G. F. Pollard, for instance, attacks Scholasticism for its lack of a vital mystical and existential dimension. Professor H. P. R. Finberg has a go at censorship. Rosemary Haughton contributes a sentitive essay on "Freedom and the Individual." The omnipresent Archbishop Roberts speaks again on the inadequacy of the Church's recent teaching on war and contraception. The escalation in those essays, however, is gentle. It is not at all gentle in the opening piece, "Some Reflections on Superstition and Credulity," by Magdalen Goffin. Mrs. Goffin rails against a magical notion of religion, an old enough target, but along the way she manages to say "To believe in eternal punishment is superstitious. . . ." *That* is escalation, and of the most effective kind, building as it does on a number of other reservations which would not bother most educated Catholics. When *Objections* first appeared in England, it was roundly assaulted, most notably by Evelyn Waugh; and numerous reviewers pointed to the "dubious orthodoxy" of Mrs. Goffin's essay. Yet so far as I know nothing happened to Mrs. Goffin; she was no more bitterly castigated than any number of other writers of recent years. In short, her escalation of the discussion of superstition was a success.

Needless to say, it is precisely this kind of development which feeds the anxieties and forebodings of many, and not just those reactionaries who had opposed the Council and all its works from the start. A notable feature of Catholic life in recent months has been a reaction even on the part of many once fully identified with the drive for *aggiornamento.* There are warnings about "going too far." There are objections to the seemingly nasty tone of much Catholic debate. There are admonitions to "slow down." When a Monsignor John Tracy Ellis feels compelled to chide some lay speakers and writers, as he did recently, then clearly the reaction can't summarily be dismissed as a sign of hard-shell Catholicism showing its old face once again. "Where will it all end?" The question is one which the "new freedom" was bound to raise; the only surprise is that it has been so long in coming.

The question is sensible and it should be taken seriously. One might begin with a few of the most common worries. It has been said, for instance, that the tone of some lay writing has of late shown a tendency toward real disrespect for authority, and at least has manifested a lack of elementary courtesy and charity. I see no reason why this should be denied. One can, without much trouble, find scattered pieces of evidence to support the charge, and even more if one reads between the lines (a legitimate though hazardous, enterprise). Yet there are some extenuating circumstances which explain why it is not always easy, or even desirable, to speak and write in the genteel language the anti-critics want. The most significant is the fact of continuing abuses on the part of a few bishops, some provincials, and many chancery functionaries. In such cases, there is no course other than harsh denunciation; the quiet, well-modulated complaint seems to do no good at all. An aroused public opinion is highly effective and necessary in the Church; it can't always be had with the rhetoric of rectory tea parties.

Another extenuating circumstance is that, by and large, the bishops and functionaries are distant, almost abstract figures to most of those who write and give lectures. It takes a powerful effort of the imagination to visualize a bishop one has never met, and probably never could meet, as another human being with feelings and hard-won views. Direct and intimate conversations, human contacts among bishops and laymen and bishops and untitled priests are exceedingly rare; hence when a bishop is attacked he is attacked as a figurehead. There is nothing personal in all of this. How could there be when the bishop as a person is often unknown? This is one of the prices we pay for a Church which is cumbersomely large, little marked by a living sense of community, and weighted down with a combination of medieval etiquette and modern, impersonal bureaucracy. In his small book *Priest and People* (Sheed & Ward, 1965), Father Joseph H.

Fichter, S.J., discovered that fifty percent of the priests he sur-
veyed from the largest metropolitan centers felt that their bishop
took little or no interest in them. One can sympathize with the
bishops, whose domain is often a complex ecclesiastical empire, far
more than one man could be expected to administer in a direct
and intimate way; but the statistic is still painful beyond words.
No wonder that so many arguments can be carried on only in the
public press, where words and not people are dominant.

Still another consideration is that of the general quest for a
fresh way of talking about the Church and talking in the Church.
The desire for a vernacular language is by no means restricted to
the liturgy; it cuts through every dimension of Catholic discourse.
Just as the current translations of the Mass are marked by much
clumsiness, so too the rhetoric of debate has by no means found
its natural idiom. Until such time as the Catholic writer, lecturer,
and debater finds a mode of expression both strong and yet still
Christian, linguistic excesses will continue to prevail.

Is any of this dangerous? Well, one has to ask: dangerous
to what? It is not necessarily dangerous to the sense of friendship
and mutual personal respect which is supposed to exist between
authority and subject. That friendship and respect has for some
time often been only a mere formality, a victim of impersonal
structures and lack of personal contact. The vigorous writing of
recent months only makes what was once hidden publicly visible.
It is not dangerous to the office of authority, for no one has
directly questioned the rights of office; only the romance of
authority may suffer, and there is no harm there. Nor is it dangerous to the more simple folk among the laity who, it is sometimes
said, are not capable of making the kinds of subtle distinctions
native to intellectuals. Whoever these "simple folk" are, they live
in the world too and as often as not have the same problems as
any other Catholic.

Most of the backlash, then, with all its attendant nervousness,
has been misdirected. Much of it seems based on a belief that the
Church will inevitably go to pieces if the politeness and dishonest
discretion of old gives way to a different style of talk and argument.

The only piece of evidence which might tend to support this assumption is the course of the contraception debate. No doubt the many unsanctioned books and articles questioning the prohibition of contraceptives have seriously undermined whatever little respect there may once have been for the teaching of Pius XI and XII. But here one can only say that, again, it was a matter of articulating reservations which were widely known but unspoken. Nothing really new was added, unless it be the positive efforts to find the basis for a development of doctrine.

Still, it would be naïve to deny the possibility of any dangers in the "new freedom." Revolutionaries have ever been known to go berserk once free of their chains and no species of self-righteousness can be as strong as that felt by former prisoners jailed unjustly; so too there is an ever-present temptation to choose whatever means lie easily at hand to carry out reforms. To mention first the most obvious seduction: commercialism. Part of the drama of Vatican II and its aftermath can look like that of a dark jail cell being blown apart by the prisoners inside. There is a good story there, and one is well paid to tell it these days. If he is better than average at the game, he can be assured of publicity and prominence. The most flagrant example of the possibilities here is *Ramparts* magazine. A combination of vulgarized reform zeal and ingenious hucksterism, *Ramparts* is scant on theological substance. Apparently that is not really so important, at least if one is to judge by the words of its editor, Mr. Edward Keating. He is quoted on the fly leaf of his book, *The Scandal of Silence* (Random House, 1965), as saying "It is not so much what is said as it is the fact that something at all was said." To the extent that there are many in the Church who feel the need for a catharsis (any old kind), he may have a point. But there is no future in this at all. It makes for a good press conference, but does little for reform. There has been a "scandal of silence" in the Church. Mr. Keating is perfectly correct there, and he succeeds in popularizing some of its causes and cures in his book. Yet the total effect is only to prove there can be as much scandal in diffuse noise as in perpetual silence. A Catholic David Susskind is no answer to the Fulton J. Sheens. At about the same time *Ramparts* began, so did *Continuum*, a superb quarterly. Almost everyone has now heard of *Ramparts*, but few know of *Continuum*. *Ramparts* has reaped the rewards which come of trivializing serious matters; *Continuum*, blessedly, has standards and intellectual rigor, which of course rarely make the news.

Another danger is that, in our enthusiasm for reform, we will let approaches and arguments go by which should be criticized. A case in point is Anne Biezanek's book, *All Things New* (Harper & Row, 1965). Dr. Biezanek recounts in her book the mental anguish and abuse she has suffered over her inability to accept the Holy See's prohibition of contraceptives. Her story is a painful one to hear, and it is understandable why she felt driven to open a family planning clinic in England. Doubtless the open expression of her problems is one more piece of useful evidence, for those who will listen, that the Church should leave the means of family planning in the hands of individual couples. In that respect *All Things New* is, as one says these days, "courageous and deeply moving" (*Birmingham Post*). It also happens to contain some of the silliest theology seen in a long time. Dr. Biezanek couples her plea for an acceptance of contraceptives with an equally fervent hope that the Church will define as a dogma the notion that Mary is the Co-Redemptrix. "It is my belief," she writes, "that the recent spectacular advance in contraceptive knowledge is a *sign from heaven* . . . a sign . . . that Eve is now truly forgiven [and] . . . that the reprieve for the daughters of Eve was won for them by 'the second Eve,' Mary. . . ." "The contraceptive pill has come to woman as a heavenly reprieve from . . . primordial doom." Just as the Church has not had the courage to change its teaching on contraception, so it has cravenly been steering clear of Mariology recently for reasons of ecumenical "expediency."

Should one go out of one's way to note such things about a book which serves a good cause? Doesn't one provide the moss-backs with ammunition by calling attention to the more bizarre aspects of Dr. Biezanek's argument? The questions have a familiar ring about them: they are the same kind of questions asked by

those who would have the Church hide its sins and faults, who
panic that some revelation of stupidity will harm the Church's
public image. Enough of such questions; they are as wrong from
one quarter as from another. To the extent that the new freedom
can bring itself to look hard at its own by-products, dealing harshly
with them if necessary, will it save itself from dishonesty. The
atmosphere of the new freedom has made it possible for the
Biezaneks and the Keatings to speak; they and others like them
need that freedom. But the freedom will not be complete until
there is no sense of hesitation in criticizing what they say, no
worries about setting back "the cause," no doubts about the wisdom
of rejecting would-be allies.

Two more dangers should be noted. Just as harsh papal denunciations and excommunications seem to have gone out of
style, so also fewer and fewer seem to feel a need to dramatically
break with the Church. Reformers have become too wise to pack up
and leave the Church; the Church has become too wise to drive
them out. I count this the greatest blessing of the new freedom.
There is breathing room now in the Church; there is room for
what the Anglican Bishop of Woolwich, John A. T. Robinson,
has called "our private discounts and transpositions." But as so
often happens the greatest blessing entails the greatest risk: the
very real possibility that we would each come to create our private
little church-within-the-Church, with our own idiosyncratic creed
and commitments. No one but ourselves need know of the existence of these private enclaves, so it is safe enough business. Yet
I think in the long run it would be the very death of theological
progress and personal integrity. There is no greater need today
than to find out what the essence of Christianity is. This must
be a communal task; the easy way out is to give it our own
meaning. To find our own way of appropriating Christianity is one
thing; to stuff it with our own contents is quite another. The
former is necessary, the latter can be disastrous.

A word should be said about recriminations and purges. There
are none so noxious to reformers as faint-hearted brethren, wor-
riers, and doubters. The desire for a revolutionary purity of vision,

a total commitment, is a grand thing; it also leads to witch-hunts, the obsessive sniffling out of potential defectors, the repudiation of former friends who give evidence of going soft. This could easily happen in the atmosphere of the new freedom, precisely because its spirit is so powerful and yet still not fully established. Can we in the Church resist this spirit? The signs so far are not wholly favorable, at least to judge from some enraged indignation directed of late at Monsignor Ellis and Justus Lawler, to mention only a couple of names. If we are going to use the word "courage," we had better not forget that it often takes more nerve to differ with one's friends than with the outside enemy establishment. Nor should we forget that to differ is not to betray.

Now none of this has answered the question raised earlier about the new freedom: where will it all end? The answer, I want to suggest, is that the question can't possibly be answered, and that it is a waste of time to try. This much at least can be said: the new freedom is here to stay. Not all the condemnations that any anxious pope or bishop could pronounce, nor any new *Syllabus of Errors* or neo-Modernist oath, would make more than a momentary difference. They would simply be swallowed up, for the new freedom is not just limited to a small, controllable elite, but is a genuine movement of the people, springing from a sudden and wholly unexpected vision of what the Church can become, of what it must no longer be. The vision is cloudy, the efforts fumbling. Yet there is power and life.

There are moments in history when, so to speak, the Church must become "the new Church." This is now happening; that is the meaning of the new freedom. For those who worry about escalation, about bringing more and more traditional positions under scrutiny, there can be no easy word of comfort. The Church has rapidly passed beyond a desire only for renewal of existing forms and doctrines; it is now coming to ask who God is, what faith is, what the Church is. These are the root questions. They are the ones we have been trying to ask all along, without quite knowing how. Is this "going too far"? Where else can one go without risking the loss of everything? The loss of meaning, of conviction, of direction, of love, of God Himself. That is what is at stake with the new freedom, and it is frightening. Or at least it will be so for those who do not see the hand of the Holy Spirit. For those who do, there can be fear as well; but joy will drive it out. At last.

CHAPTER SEVENTEEN

The Logic of Religion

WHILE IT IS NOW GENERALLY AGREED THAT CHRISTIANITY IS undergoing a crisis, it is not at all evident just what lies behind it. Is it a matter of the "relevance" of Christianity? Or of a widespread loss of a sense of the supernatural? Or is it perhaps only a by-product of the inevitable difficulties of translating biblical perspectives into contemporary terms? Each of these explanations has much to commend it, and they are even more plausible if taken together as part of a complex whole. Even so there is still something missing.

I want to suggest, in a very tentative way, that Christianity in general, and many of the churches in particular, lack today a clear sense of their own logic. This suggestion requires some explanation and presupposes certain assumptions. Let me state some of my assumptions: 1) few believers can for long tolerate a lack of order, system, and coherence in their religious beliefs;

2) few churches can for long tolerate mutually incompatible theologies, incompatible stances toward the world, and incompatible
understandings of their purpose and mission; 3) for the sake of
their long-term health, both individual believers and the churches
require a reasonably well-ordered and well-articulated set of convictions. Where these minimal conditions are lacking, at least over
the long run, the result will be one form or another of disintegration.
The individual believer will soon show signs of neuroticism, becoming irritable, inconsistent in his conduct, prone to destructive
criticism, and wildly erratic in his emotional life (ecstatic one
moment, depressed the next). He will, in other words, feel and act
like a man who has lost his bearings. Something of the same kind
will happen in the churches: they will be rent by violent disputes,
by the formation of sharply antagonistic factions, even by heresies
and schisms; one way or another they will lose their sense of unity
and community.

Many of these neurotic symptoms are now present, though
so far in a relatively mild form. But I think it can safely be
predicted that the symptoms will grow more pronounced, and
very quickly, if Christianity does not succeed in articulating a
fresh logic. Now a natural question at this point might be: what
was the old logic and what has happened to it? Unfortunately,
the question is misleading. It is doubtful that Christianity has
ever been marked by a single logic or a single and orderly set of
beliefs. Instead, the history of Christianity shows that many alternative systems of Christian belief have developed. There have
been rationalistic theologies and mystical theologies, secular theologies and ascetical theologies, history-centered theologies and
philosophy-centered theologies. Each has had its own methods,
modes of reasoning, and characteristic marks. Sometimes the
conflicts among these alternatives led to disaster; more often one
or the other would gain sway. It was then possible for the individual or for a church to work with a mode of belief which had
an inner coherence, a logic. Everything could be put in place, at
least in a general way; consensus could be achieved because of a
shared framework.

The trouble at our present point in history is that no single system of belief or ordered set of perspectives has achieved this kind of dominance. The present state of Catholic thought is a natural example. Until perhaps the middle of the twentieth century, a rationalistic theology held sway. Whatever its deficiencies in detail, it had an aesthetically and intellectually attractive coherence. The virtues of this system were many: there would be no conflict between faith and reason, because what reason could not supply the Church could; there need be no crises of belief because the evidence for the validity of Christ's revelation was incontrovertible (miracles, prophecies, etc.); there would be little uncertainty about living the Christian life because the Church had decisively spelled out the rules.

What happened to this tidy arrangement? The philosophers chipped away by showing that it is not so easy, after all, to establish God's existence solely by reason. The theologians came to doubt whether a rationalistic theology does justice to the centrality of faith and the reality of mystery. The biblicists showed that Scripture does not reveal a set of true propositions, but rather the person of Christ and the history of salvation. The Council Fathers asserted in the *Constitution on the Church* that God does not reveal Himself only through the medium of hierarchical authority, but also directly to the individual through the promptings of the Holy Spirit. And papal infallibility? It is a grand doctrine, except that hardly anyone seems able to set down a list of those occasions on which the Pope has undeniably spoken infallibly. Finally, the moral theologians have rejected the notion that the Church can or should lay down a complete set of moral laws. All of this doesn't quite demolish the older theology, but it leaves a tottering structure, daily dropping bits and pieces of debris. From the viewpoint of the reformer, this is perfectly grand; the sooner the old building collapses the better.

Yet one has to ask what is being built in its place. If my earlier assumptions are correct, *some* kind of new logical *structure* must rise; or, if you will, a new system must be created. For the time being, the Church may be able to get by on a few key concepts, salvation-history, the Word, encounter, people of God, loosely knitting them together into a charismatic whole. But in the long run, these concepts will have to issue in a full-blown, fully organized theology. I say this, in a sense, despite myself. One of the truly exciting things about our era is the loss of a passion for beautiful systems. There is a willingness to accept isolated glimmers of truth, incomplete results, and tentative probings. In the Church this has taken the form, above all, of an openness to the Holy Spirit, a belief that God can break in on man in wholly unexpected ways, that man's theological system can prove to be wholly defective in the face of a blinding light from God. Just as philosophy needed to throw off the disease of Hegelianism in the early decades of this century, so too the Church needed to throw off the disease of a geometric theology.

Yet the confusion which results is enormous. One can, of course, try to make the instability itself an asset; hence, one praises the value of taking risks, of making anguished decisions, of walking in the dark. But clearly this stance does not do sufficient justice to the equally important biblical themes of Christian joy, peace, and redemption. Moreover, if some people can thrive on dark nights of the soul it is doubtful that most human beings can —or at any rate, can do so indefinitely. Somehow, in some way, they have to find a way of ordering the universe and of ordering their religious life. In some way, they have to be provided with a theological system which integrates a broad variety of experiences, convictions, and outlooks. It does not matter that the system may be provisional—ideally, it should be.

A good system would be one marked by flexibility, by the possibility of encompassing many diverse insights and directions; it would be inclusive rather than exclusive. But a good system also requires a logical backbone. It must have at least a few fundamental principles, some fixed points of reference (e.g., central themes in the Bible, confessional or creedal statements, or even perhaps meta-scriptural slogans such as *sola fide, sola scriptura,* and so on). What is important, from the logical point of view, is not the contents of principles or fixed points as such, but that there be some in the first place. No less important, again from the logical point of view, is that there be some consistent norms for the use of language, some reasonably clear criteria whereby one can determine what may be included in the system and what may not, and the possibility of discerning the implications of any given affirmation for the system as a whole and for the life of the person who would make it his own.

All of this, I recognize, is terribly abstract; indeed, considerations of this kind may seem obnoxious, as if I am sneaking by the back door once again into the too-brightly lit room of rationalistic, mystery-denying theology. Does not an openness to the Word entail the destruction of our human logics? Must we not admit that the Holy Spirit may touch us in ways which confound our expectations, our grasp of concepts (for instance: "love"), our painfully achieved certainties? I think the answer has to be: only up to a point. Unless we have some way of integrating even the most revolutionary incursions of the Holy Spirit into some preexisting framework, we are not likely to know whether it *is* the Holy Spirit who touches us. Abraham was ready to slay Isaac at God's command—to "suspend the ethical" in Kierkegaard's terms. Obviously God was confounding Abraham in the most radical way. Yet however insane or inhuman God's command may have seemed, it *was* God's command. And Abraham knew— in a context still broader than the ethical—that it made sense to obey God. That was his guiding principle. Put in my terms, there was a logic to Abraham's system of belief; thus one can see why he was willing to obey, however senseless the particular command may have seemed.

Now it should be evident, though perhaps not, that questions about the logic of religion or the logic of theological systems will in great part be meta-religious and meta-theological. This was borne in on me at least by Father Joseph Bochenski's short book *The Logic of Religion* (New York University Press, 1965). What he tries to do in the book is to apply symbolic logic to religious discourse and concepts. He wants to see what their logical structure is, what laws they follow, what kind of linguistic transformations they permit or exclude. For one caught up in much contemporary theology his project may seem sterile beyond words; to talk of the living God as "('x) (ψx)" where, in Bochenski's words "'ψ' is substituted for the product of the predicates attributed to God by the creeds" is not likely to induce "meeting" or "encounter." But to do what he wanted to, Father Bochenski had to go outside of religion and theology; neither is easily able, in itself, to reveal its own logic. Or even if they are, they can be further illuminated by employing very human tools and analytical devices. Beyond that, Father Bochenski is trying to show how crucial it is that we find some way of discerning logical structures. If we are not able to, we open ourselves to many kinds of absurdity. (Father Bochenski is particularly effective in showing the drawbacks of theologies which try to build on the notion of "paradox.")

Unfortunately, very few these days are interested in such matters. Jean Guitton touched on the logic of religion in *The Problem of Jesus*; John Wilson has written a small book, *Philosophy and Religion: The Logic of Religious Belief*; and Ninian Smart made a contribution in *Reasons and Faiths*. There are other books as well, but not many. Almost every one has been written by a philosopher rather than a theologian, and they have concentrated more on religion in the broadest sense than on recent theological speculation. The field is ready for harvest.

No Final Word

TRADITIONALLY, A COLLECTION OF ESSAYS HAS ATTACHED TO IT an afterword, often enough pulling together loose strings, neatly trying the package, and then, as a final touch, soaring to the rhetorical heavens to deliver an ultimate prophetic word. I can do none of these things. The loose strings are too plentiful, the package would leak, and I do not have an ecstatic word. I constantly marvel at the oracular books and articles on religion which daily flow from the presses. Their authors are to be envied, for vision is not easy to come by these days. No one, at least, has supplied me with any. But I am willing to settle for something less grand: just to get the problems straight so that others can go on to extract the vision.

An observant reader, however, might well object that on occasion my own rhetoric smacks more of the oracular than I seem willing to concede myself. But isn't that the way it usually

212

works out? Like many others, I write and, at the moment of creation, visions dance in my head. Ah, but months later it is a different story: gaps appear, the illogic surfaces, the moment has passed. So at least I usually respond to my own visions recollected in dull tranquillity.

Some of the problems are still there, though—and some are not. To mention the latter first, let me begin with ecumenism and pluralism. Though a reversal is still conceivable, it is not too dangerous to say that ecumenism and pluralism are ceasing to be critical problems in the Church. Just why this has happened so quickly is not altogether clear. My own guess is that the rapid social assimilation of Catholics in the past decade accounts for much of the change. If it is still possible for a Catholic to feel alienated along the lines indicated in my opening essay, his alienation is even more likely to take different forms now. No longer is he so likely to find non-Catholic intellectuals rejecting him out of hand; in many places he is actively courted. Nor is he so likely to find the Catholic community hostile to his probings and aspirations; he has actually become something of a hero since the Council. Now and again, he will meet rebuffs, but he is learning to take them in stride.

Ecumenism has found a surprisingly ready acceptance in the Church simply because Catholics and Protestants have come to know each other much better in the past ten years. They are no longer so fearful. Many of the earlier dilemmas of pluralism are rapidly vanishing because Catholics and non-Catholics are learning how to share the same government and the same society and how to work their way through to a reasonable consensus on issues of public policy. Protestants, for instance, are now a good deal more permissive when federal or state money finds its way into the parochial school system. And Catholics are equally permissive in the face of non-Catholic attempts to change state laws on divorce, birth control, and Sunday blue laws. On occasion, the fur will still fly, but almost everyone has learned to live with these periodic fracases. They are now taken as part of the game and not the signal for eternal anathemas and irreparable breaks.

Even more significant, disputed questions are likely to cut across confessional lines. Should America be thought of as a "religious" nation? Should a "secular" society become the new ideal? Should the churches support the war in Vietnam? Should ministers of the Lord take part in public demonstrations and protests? There are many answers to these questions, but only rarely do they take the form of "Catholic" or "Protestant" answers.

George Lindbeck of the Yale Divinity School observed a few years back that Protestant and Catholic ecumenists in Europe often have more in common with each other than with their own sectarian brethren. The same is now happening in this country, and the phenomenon is extending into civil rights, theologies of secularity, the response to urbanization, nuclear war, and Communism. Harvey Cox has speculated that the important religious struggles of the future will be between "worldly" and "religious" Christians, each to be found in all churches, rather than in denominational battles. That distinction is a bit too neat and imprecise, but something of the kind is indeed making its appearance. In Catholicism, signs can be detected of a sharp difference between those pragmatically oriented and analytically inclined, and those seeking a new synthesis and an overarching quasimystical grasp of the whole; again, this dichotomy can also be found in other churches. The almost-desperate campaign to demythologize or rapidly reinterpret what are taken to be the "traditional" theological concepts and beliefs of the churches again admits of no denominational boundaries. If Protestants have had more practice here than Catholics, it is still an uncomfortable business for almost everyone. There are not a few who wonder whether these frantic lifesaving measures will work; and not a few who feel perpetually guilty because they even feel compelled to try. There are fewer and fewer smug Christians to be found these days, especially those confident about the grasp their particular church has on the truth. More and more, the significant theological questions are Christian questions, not "Catholic" or "Protestant" questions.

Why is this happening? We are discovering how hard it is

to know what Christianity really is and to know what it is to live a Christian life. This discovery has been forced on Christians both from the inside and from the outside. From the inside, the vast amount of theological, philosophical, and biblical research of the past few decades is shattering almost all the old certainties. From the outside, social change, historical movement, the rise of technology, psychoanalytic techniques, vast political upheavals, have all conspired to place the Churches and the Christian in a wholly unfamiliar setting. Both the inner Christian world and the outer secular world are changing at the same time, and both act as catalysts for the other. In the past, when theological certainties reigned supreme, most of the tensions were generated by the outer world. That caused trouble enough, but at least there was a solid religious core from which to work. I myself, not untypically, was raised to believe that the main task for the contemporary Christian was to apply unchanging truths to changing social and intellectual "challenges." Now one has to cope with a changing grasp of Christian truth at the same time, to "apply" that which is changing to something else which is also changing.

One result has been to unmask many of these earlier confidences: too many sprung from shallow roots, superficial scholarship, and the abiding attraction of superstition. When the world finally got into the Church (mainly as a result of education and social assimilation) the old certitudes could not stand the exposure, the interrogation, and the altered milieu which the world brought with it. All the pointed questions raised by the Renaissance, the Enlightenment, and the explosion of the nineteenth century, questions which the churches had managed to evade, could be escaped no longer. Now they are smashing home, and new ones are constantly being added. Ironically, the more successful the churches become in taking the world seriously, in "getting out" into the world, the more they will be forced to answer basic questions about their ultimate meaning. The psychological and institutional benefits of ghettoism should not be underestimated. They enabled the Church to maintain an inner consistency and harmony, a persistent loyalty, and provided its members with a fixed conception of what they must believe and do. Once the walls come down, disorder and confusion are inevitable: the sources of value become diffused, there remains no single center of loyalty, and self-identity must be fashioned from a variety of possible images and models. Inexorably, anyone who would call himself a Christian today is forced to ask questions which had, so he had been told, already been answered.

For the Catholic, the only condition under which these basic questions can once again be asked is that of personal and institutional freedom. Who is God? How are we to speak of Him? And Christ, who is He? What is man and what are we to make of him? The Church? The sacraments? Worship? Papal and episcopal authority? Infallibility? The Church needs the freedom to ask questions of this kind, more freedom than it has known for centuries, more than even seems conceivable for it. It needs to be free of the distractions of pluralistic bickering, of useless disunities, of institutional inanities. "The new freedom" of which I spoke earlier is imperative.

Yet I deliberately chose to place that essay next to "The Logic of Religion." For I am equally convinced that the "new freedom" has not yet produced anything in the way of a new logic. If this logic is not forthcoming, the freedom will only have been the mark of the Church's dissolution, liberating perhaps to many individuals, but productive of little substantive content. I, for one, would be perfectly willing to see the ruination of the Church if that was the price necessary for personal freedom. For if it is through freedom—that freedom God gave man as his most precious possession—that we come to Christ and thus to the Church, it makes no sense to curtail that freedom for the sake of the Church. A freedom which is necessary and valuable prior to commitment to Christ and the Church does not cease to be valuable and necessary once that commitment has been made. Yet eventually there has to be order. Not the superficial "good order" ecclesiastical authorities sometimes extoll, an "order" much like martial law in a beseiged city. Not that order which would suppress discussion for the sake of the simple faithful. Not that order whereby everyone is given his proper niche, out of which he steps only at his peril.

I am thinking rather of that inner order necessary for mental, spiritual, and emotional stability. Man can live in a disorderly world. He can even live without a clear understanding of what the world and the cosmos mean. But he cannot live without some kind of inner harmony, without coming to terms with himself. Nor can a Christian community live if it does not come to terms with itself. Neither the person nor the community can for long endure an inner shambles. And that, I feel compelled to say, is what Christianity is coming to—because of the pointed and often unanswerable questions being put to it by the world, and because of the questions which its own theological research and speculations are raising.

The "new freedom," which is the only hope for eventual order, is at the same time a major source of the disorder. Anyone who overlooks the second half of that equation, letting his enthusiasm run away with him, will be missing the obvious. Despite a culture saturated with psychoanalysis, which has a sharp eye for social and historical determinism, and which makes much of unmasking self-hypocrisy and self-deceit, Christians still have difficulty in taking a straight look at themselves. This is as true of the passionate defenders of the "new freedom" as it is of those who oppose it. Without any trouble at all, one could sketch out a perfectly plausible case that the new Christian defenders of freedom are just as much victims of the culture as those Christian reactionaries they oppose. The point is not that they should, for this reason, give up their quest for freedom, but that they have the capacity to see where they themselves are more cultural products than self-products. This is (so we usually think) easy enough to do with others: we can observe them, scribble notes on our little analysts' pad, and then confidently consign them to their proper pigeonhole. How we hate to do that in our own case: "I'm too complex, too rich, too sensitive, too subtle, too contradictory; no one can categorize me." And it is true. But we are still not the pure self-directing creatures we like to imagine ourselves, not quite.

With what, then, are we left? Freedom, yes. Order, yes. Commitment to the Church, yes. Commitment to the destruction of the Church if that is necessary for freedom, yes. You see, the strings can't be tied together, after all. Yes, yes to everything. And no, too. No, to those visions which make us think we have, finally, at last, at last, placed a pin through our precious piece of truth. No, to those rantings whereby we throw people off cliffs and shout that they are now free. No, to alienation, old and new.

Tie all this together in a beautiful afterword? Tell me how.

I will just say that out of this turmoil, these contradictions, there must somehow come a new Church. Now I see it; now I don't. But come it must.

Index